# LAFAYETTE,
## WE ARE HERE!

## Jean-Michel Steg

Foreword by Jay Winter

Translated by Ethan Rundell

UNIVERSITY OF
**BUCKINGHAM**
PRESS

Published by University of Buckingham Press,
an imprint of Legend Times Group
51 Gower Street
London WC1E 6HJ
info@unibuckinghampress.com
www.unibuckinghampress.com

First published in French in 2018 by Éditions Fayard

© Jean-Michel Steg, 2018, 2022
Translation © Ethan Rundell, 2018

ISBN (paperback): 9781915054685
ISBN (ebook): 9781915054692

Cover design: Ditte Løkkegaard

*For E., R. and G.*

## I Have a Rendezvous with Death

At some disputed barricade
When Spring comes back with rustling shade
And apple blossoms fill the air –
I have a rendezvous with Death
When Spring brings back blue days and fair.

Alan Seeger (1888–1916)

# CONTENTS

Foreword by Jay Winter...........................................................................1

Preface....................................................................................................5

Introduction.........................................................................................11
'Lafayette, We Are Here!'

Chapter 1.............................................................................................18
Belleau Wood, 6 June 1918, Dawn

Chapter 2.............................................................................................28
6 June 1918, 17.00: The Attack

Chapter 3.............................................................................................34
The Battle of Belleau Wood Rages On

Chapter 4.............................................................................................48
Early 1917: The State of the Conflict on the Eve of the United
States' Entry into the War

Chapter 5.............................................................................................51
Why Didn't the United States Enter the War in August 1914?

Chapter 6.............................................................................................61
The American Army before It Entered the War

Chapter 7.............................................................................................64
The United States Slides into War

**Chapter 8**................................................................................73
The German General Staff's Strategic Gamble

**Chapter 9**................................................................................80
Preparing the American Intervention

**Chapter 10**..............................................................................92
The German Spring Offensive of 1918 and the American
Baptism of Fire

**Chapter 11**............................................................................102
What Was the True Military Impact of the Battle of
Belleau Wood?

**Chapter 12**............................................................................107
The Last Hundred Days of the War

**Chapter 13**............................................................................116
After the Armistice, then the Treaty of Versailles

**Chapter 14**............................................................................123
War's End for the United States

**Post-Mortem**.........................................................................130

**Bibliography**.........................................................................135

**Acknowledgements**................................................................137

**Endnotes**..............................................................................139

# FOREWORD

## THE ARRIVAL OF THE AMERICANS, 1917-18

There has been an avalanche of historical writing published during the centenary of the outbreak of the Great War. And yet there is still one major omission remaining to be filled with respect to every front and every theatre of military operations. In short, the year 1918 is in need of attention.

Surprisingly, we still have no major account as to how the great stalemate of 1914–17 was broken, and why the strategic advantages the Central Powers held in late 1917 vanished a year later. These are still open questions, in part because of the complexity and transnational reach of the war. It is clear that the reasons why one side won are different from the reasons the other side lost, but a measured account of both is still to be written.

Jean-Michel Steg has provided a way forward in his multi-level account of the arrival of the Americans in the last year of the war. First, we see the war from the bottom up. Steg offers a splendid narrative of the taking of Belleau Wood by the US Marines in early June 1918. We see the confusion alongside the courage of the men on both sides and watch at eye level as the US Marine Corps breathes life into a legend which lasts to this day.

Secondly, we see the war from the top down and come to locate nasty encounters like Belleau Wood within the framework of the turning point of the war, separating the stalemate of 1914–17 from the war of movement and endgame of 1918.

Above all, Steg shows us that American entry into the Great War in April 1917 did not end it. What the United States did in 1917 was to prolong the war, at a time when Russia was in revolutionary turmoil and when Britain and France were stretched, almost to the breaking point, both in terms of manpower and financial power.

US help in stabilizing the Allied cause was of even greater significance in 1918. What the United States did was to present to the German army and government in 1918 a terrible prospect for the future. When the March 1918 offensive failed, what they could no longer ignore was the likelihood of facing 3 million more American troops in the very near future. Thus it was not American power on the Western Front in 1918 but the projection of American power into 1919 and 1920 that made the difference to both Allied and German thinking about which side would win and which side would not win the war. For the German high command, that recognition came late, in the summer of 1918, and not one second before. Their monumental arrogance is well known and so is their underestimation of the ability of the United States to project its power overseas. They made the same mistake twenty-five years later.

We see that the anticipation of future massive injections of American troops into the lines mattered to the Allies, too, since the longer the war went on, the more the United States would be able to dictate the terms of the peace. As an 'associated' power rather than an Ally, America's voice was strong but not dominant in 1917. By the autumn of 1918, British and French forces were exhausted, giving to the United States a greater and greater role both in the way the war was fought and in the way the peace would be drafted. For Britain and France, the time for an armistice had arrived in November 1918, before the Americans took over the war; General John J. Pershing, the American commander, thought otherwise and planned a thrust into Germany in late 1918 and early 1919. He was overruled by Marshal Ferdinand Foch, commander of all Allied forces, who thereby preserved a balance among the victorious powers, which lasted (just about) until the Peace Treaty was signed on 28 June 1919. This war among America's allies about who would frame the peace is one we cannot neglect in our understanding of how and when the war ended.

Once again, Steg's account provides a fresh account of this crucial period in international history. He shows that the American army did not win the war. The performance of American forces on the field of battle was mixed. The open warfare ordained by the American approach to battle never happened, although American power mattered, especially in set encounters like Belleau Wood, and, even more importantly, in the Meuse–Argonne offensive. The use of tanks was only marginally successful in the muddy and broken terrain of the Western Front, turning Patton's incipient Tank Corps into fixed artillery. In this way, Steg shows that the Americans were just as perplexed as their allies as to how to adjust their thinking about war to the novel conditions of the Western Front.

We see too that under French command, American forces – including African American forces – performed well in filling gaps in the line. Under American command, African American soldiers were treated like coolies, lest they get 'uppity' and be 'ruined' before their return to segregated America.

The bottom line is that, on the whole, US units operated

just like French and British units in 1915–16. They had to undergo a 'learning curve', which wound up as a 'bleeding curve', especially in the last four months of the war. Then US forces were hit by the Spanish flu – indeed, it is possible that they brought it with them. One of the centres of incubation and dissemination of the mutant virus was the major American army base at Fort Leavenworth in Kansas. Doughboys died by the thousands even before they got their travel orders to sail across the Atlantic, but then millions of men on both sides of the lines joined the long list of victims of this mutant viral infection.

We owe Jean-Michel Steg a vote of gratitude for giving us his insights not only on the last phase of the Great War but also on the way the Great War left its mark on the American way of war. Many of the leading players in the Second World War – MacArthur, Patton, Marshall, Truman – had their baptism of fire in industrial warfare in 1917–18. What they learned informed what they did in their later careers. The long shadow of 1917–18 in France reaches well into the second half of the twentieth century and beyond. Its traces linger still.

Jay Winter

# PREFACE

A century on, the First World War continues stubbornly to hold our attention. The media is replete with stories of commemorations, pilgrimages and old or recently discovered first-person accounts. The exceptional persistence of the war's memory is a reflection of its extraordinary human cost. It seems to have left a sort of after-image in the collective memory of successive generations, testimony to the huge physical and mental toll it inflicted on a vast proportion of the warring countries' male populations.[1]

Although organized violence has been part of the documented history of the Western world since at least the Bronze Age, the level of lethality attained in the early twentieth century represented a catastrophic novelty. Two factors explain this unanticipated spike of mass death in combat.

First, the very rapid and extensive technological progress of the late nineteenth century resulted in near exponential growth in the firepower and destructive capacity of weaponry. Next, the advent of the industrial era and the simultaneous expansion of production, infrastructure and restrictive social norms allowed armies of several million men to be assembled and transported to the battlefield, sometimes literally from the other side of the world. Due to the impossibility of recruiting, equipping, transporting and feeding so many men at once, never before had any nation or ethnic group been capable of forming armies on this scale, not even in the Napoleonic Wars of a century earlier.

These fundamental changes required that military doctrine and practice be transformed, a process that proved painful, not just from the point of view of the ethos of military leaders, but also for the bodies of the soldiers under their command. The reason for this was that such adaptation ran directly counter to what had been fundamental aspects of combat since the origin of war itself. Beginning with the Bronze Age, the warrior had to be as visible as possible to his enemy. His appearance had to underscore and amplify his adversary's perception of his strength and ferocity. The crest of his helmet made him taller; the shape of his armour made him larger; his tunic was a scarlet colour, and so on. Beginning in the late nineteenth century, this tendency was rapidly reversed. Faced with enemy firepower, the foot soldier now had to seek stealth in his appearance – to disappear from enemy view. Richly coloured outfits were replaced with ones that sought to merge the wearer's silhouette with the ground (khaki), greenery (verdigris) or the sky (horizon blue). This elimination of the combatant from the field of vision was accompanied by the warlord's disappearance from the battlefield. Alexander charged the Persians at the head of his phalanxes. Henri IV asked his troops to 'rally around his white plume', which precisely made him visible to all. Several centuries later, it was still possible for Napoleon to observe the battlefield from a nearby hilltop – sufficiently close to the action to be hit in the heel by a stray bullet at Ratisbonne (1809). Henceforth, warlords would have to learn to lead their battles with the help of telephone calls received hundreds of kilometres away from the fighting.[2]

For the armies of the First World War, adapting to this new form of armed confrontation would be particularly bloody, especially at the time of their first experience of battle. From this point of view, war truly begins not with a formal declaration of war, but rather from the moment that a nation sends into fire the better part of its concentrated forces. In two earlier books, I attempted to show just how fatal it was for the troops concerned to descend the 'learning curve' of modern methods of combat.[3] By this expression, I mean the process by which an army adapts to a new conflict at the level of its organization and operation, which have often been shaped by earlier (more or less recent, more or less similar) wars. This forced adaptation gets underway with the first large-scale confrontation with the enemy and has consequences for all involved, from the men of the general staff and officer corps to the rank-and-file soldier. For the French armies, this 'first time' took place in late August 1914 during the Battle of the Frontiers. For their British counterparts, it would be repeated on the Somme in July 1916.

The soldiers of the American Expeditionary Corps in France would know the same fate in early summer 1918. They would in their turn go through the bloody experience that, in the early twentieth century, consisted of advancing over open ground under the enemy's combined rifle, machine-gun and artillery fire. One might have thought that American military leaders would have drawn upon the experience of their allies to reduce their losses. Quite the contrary: from the first major episodes of fighting in June 1918, American soldiers were to pay a heavy price for their leaders' apprenticeship in the methods of industrial war. Their tragic fate calls into question the real ability of any army to 'transfer experience' to another in 1914–1918, even when the armies in question are allied. Indeed, especially when they are allies, for one seems to learn more from one's enemies by simple imitation…

Nearly fifteen years ago, I had the opportunity to resume, as best I could, my studies as an historian at Paris's École des

Hautes Études en Sciences Sociales (EHESS). There, I had the good luck to work under the authority, at once scholarly and benevolent, of Stéphane Audoin-Rouzeau and in the company of an energetic and constantly changing group of young doctoral students. I have thus spent fifteen years researching the mortality spikes of this staggeringly violent war. Drawing upon masses of statistics, first-person accounts and artefacts, I have tried to extract information that might help, if not explain, then at least give some meaning to these unprecedented events.

I am of course aware of the fact that there is something unusual about devoting oneself so narrowly to the subject of mass death in combat in the early twentieth century. In particular, I am aware of the macabre nature of the subject and, were I not, the somewhat taken-aback and vaguely reproachful look of some of my interlocutors when I explain the content of my research would suffice to remind me of it. Above all, I know how vast and rich the war's history is as a subject: one may just as legitimately take an interest in its strategy, tactics, equipment, uniforms, military medicine, justice or music, and doubtless much else besides... The ability to kill other people nevertheless remains central to the subject of *combat* in wartime. And that has always been the case since men began to *recall* war. It is enough to read the songs of the *Iliad*, in which the bards clinically explain to their audience the precise impact of each striking sword blade and lance tip on the bodies of the battling Achaeans and Trojans.[4] This is why I occasionally set aside a professional or familial obligation to attend a forensic-medicine seminar or colloquium on the archaeology of communal graves on the battlefields. Despite the obvious risk of giving in, even unintentionally, to a form of voyeurism, it strikes me as difficult, if not impossible, to say much about modern war if one is unwilling to face the fact of its appalling brutality.

Alongside my general reading, seminar discussions and

research in libraries and the military archives of various armies, I have been fortunate to work on a subject that lends itself to conducting research on the field of battle itself. Over the course of recent years, I have had an opportunity to travel the length of many First World War battlefields, from Flanders and the Belgian Ardennes to a vast arc of north-eastern France. Once one has already studied the fighting that took place there, visiting sites of combat allows one to compare one's mental images with the reality on the ground. It is a very rich experience in intellectual terms but also a very powerful emotional one. For visiting the battlefields of the First World War is above all to visit individual and collective graves. There are cemeteries everywhere: small ones and large ones, massive French ossuaries, almost intimate English regimental cemeteries, white wooden French crosses, dismal black German ones, bright British stelae, communal graves, rows of individual gravestones, monuments and commemorative plaques. Everywhere one looks, the traces of death – often the death of very young men – are omnipresent.

Even today, I find it difficult to visit dispassionately the gravestones and communal graves of Rossignol in the Belgian Ardennes, where the French soldiers of the 3rd Colonial Infantry Division lie, or those of Beaumont-Hamel in the Somme, the last resting place for so many soldiers of the Newfoundland Regiment. All volunteers, these young men all died on the same day, a date repeated hundreds of times (22 August 1914 in one case, 1 July 1916 in the other). For the French and British armies, these were to be the bloodiest single days of the entire war. Standing before these communal graves, I have come to understand better how, in the *Odyssey*, Ulysses can converse with the shades of Achilles and Agamemnon without in the least 'descending' into hell. It was enough for him to find the right spot – there where the shades of the dead rise to the surface – dig a shallow pit with the tip of his sword and pour the blood of the ritual sacrifice into it.[5]

From Ypres to Les Éparges, Beaumont-Hamel to Verdun, Vimy Ridge to the Chemin des Dames and Rossignol, I have often been deeply troubled by my visits to these graves, once soaked in blood, over which wander the souls of the men who died fighting there.

It was with this same sombre and burdensome feeling that I stood before the stelae of the young American soldiers in Belleau Wood, at the border of Champagne and the Paris Basin, young men who had come to fight and die in France in the spring of 1918.

# INTRODUCTION

## 'LAFAYETTE, WE ARE HERE!'

Between June 1917 and early 1919, a wave of more than 2 million young American soldiers – many of them volunteers, most enthusiastic – debarked in the French ports of the Atlantic coast, from Brest to Bordeaux and including Nantes, Rochefort, Saint-Nazaire and La Rochelle. Inspired above all by gratitude for France's contribution 150 years earlier to the American colonies' struggle for independence, many Americans today believe that their number, equipment and energy rapidly turned the war in the Allies' favour. These soldiers came to participate in a bloody conflict that had been bogged down since the winter of 1914 and in which the most recent developments suggested that the German army – rid of its Russian adversary since the summer of 1918 – might ultimately emerge victorious. Others, however, play down the impact of the American intervention, which took place quite late in the war and, at least until the summer of 1918, had contributed relatively few troops to the front.

As is often the case, the reality of the situation demands a more nuanced approach.

First, one must take into account the fact that there was nothing inevitable about the massive participation of American troops in the First World War, which was far from automatic, much less immediate. At the start of hostilities in August 1914, the American government had taken a clear stance in favour of neutrality, and in this was overwhelmingly supported by public opinion. Over the course of the following two and a half years, there was little change in this position or in the feeling in the country. It was only after a number of major strategic miscalculations by the Germans that President Woodrow Wilson, freshly re-elected in November 1916, became convinced of the interest and need for the United States to enter the conflict. In a very short span of time, he convinced a still very divided Congress to declare war on Germany. This was accompanied by a reversal of American public opinion, with a majority (but not all) supporting a policy of active assistance for the Allied powers. For the latter, it was none too soon.

Beginning in late 1916, following the battles of Verdun and the Somme, the German general staff (now under leadership of the two-man team of General Erich Ludendorff and General Paul von Hindenburg) began to doubt the Second Reich's prospects of victory. The conflict's transformation into a war of materiel (*Materialschlacht*), particularly with the Battle of the Somme (July–November 1916), put Wilhelmine Germany in a position of inferiority. It was of course spared the devastation directly associated with fighting and territorial invasion. But its war economy faced ever greater difficulties in operating in the situation of autarchy forced upon it by the Allied blockade, the product of British naval superiority. And as time passed and the conflict wore on, the ranks of experienced German soldiers thinned while the German general staff lacked the demographic reserves available to the British and French thanks to their respective colonial empires. It was precisely this feeling that the conflict's predictable evolution did not favour them that, after much procrastination, pushed German leaders in early 1917 to opt for the resumption of all-out submarine warfare at the risk of dragging the United States into the conflict on the Allied side. In their view, the United States was hardly more inclined to enter the war in 1917 – or for that matter materially capable of doing so – than it had been in August 1914. Despite being more well disposed to the democratic regimes of Britain and France than to the Central Powers, the overwhelming majority of the American public opinion favoured neutrality in 1914. This was to remain the case even after an American ocean liner, the USS *Lusitania*, was torpedoed within sight of the Irish coast in May 1915, resulting in the death of 128 Americans (out of a total of 1,198 dead). Though it caused a media sensation, this unilateral act of war nevertheless failed to force the United States into the conflict.

Another reason for German optimism in this regard was that, in early 1917, a US army capable of fighting on the European front was no closer to being a reality than it had been in 1914. At the time, the United States lacked the rank-and-file soldiers, officers, equipment, weapons, means of transport, general staff, administrative organization and doctrine (both tactical and strategic) necessary to organize an army of several million men that would be capable of conducting modern warfare several thousand kilometres from its bases against a powerful and experienced adversary. In early 1917, Germany's leaders were thus convinced of US military unpreparedness. They believed they had ample time to break the French and the British – now potentially cut off from strategic supplies from the Americas – before American troops could intervene in Europe in any significant way.

And indeed, though the first (slim) contingents of American soldiers began to debark in France in the summer of 1917, it was only to spend many months in the training camps that the French and British armies had opened for them. In June 1917, Pershing himself arrived in France and was warmly welcomed in Paris by an enthusiastic crowd. On 4 July 1917 – American Independence Day – he travelled with his general staff to the Picpus Cemetery, where the Marquis de Lafayette lies buried. It was there that the famous expression was first heard: 'Lafayette, we are here!'[6]

Yet in reality it was only in the late spring of 1918 that American units first began to participate significantly in direct engagements against the Germans. And it was only from July – and, above all, August – that the US army was to make a major, indeed decisive contribution to the fighting in the Argonne in the last hundred days of the conflict.

It nevertheless remains the case that, beginning in early 1918, the massive and now visible arrival of US troops in France had an important impact on the morale of Allied troops and civilian populations alike. And this at a time when the exhaustion of three and a half years of unprecedentedly brutal war had begun to undermine the morale of both. By contrast, and despite their low opinion of the American soldier's fighting capacity, the inexorable influx of 'doughboys' into French ports that summer discouraged German leaders, who were already worried about their weakening demography in the aftermath of the failed offensives of spring 1918.[7] (It is true that, at the same time, the demographic deterioration of the German age cohorts available for mobilization had begun to make itself keenly felt...)

In eighteen months, American society and the American economy showed an impressive capacity to adapt to the needs generated by the country's entry into the war.

First and foremost was the need to mobilize men. A census was conducted of the male population and conscription established, resulting in the enlistment of 2.8 million men on top of the 2 million who had already volunteered, making a total of 4.8 million men in uniform.[8]

Next, there was the need to mobilize the economy at the national level, an unprecedented step for a country as decentralized and distrustful of social and economic regulation as was the United States at that time. In July 1917, for example, the War Industries Board was created to supervise the industrial system and define production priorities, as was the National War Labor Board, which oversaw wartime relations between workers and employers.

Finally, minds were mobilized, among other things via the creation of a Committee on Public Information to disseminate pro-war propaganda.[9] Alongside the use of the usual exhortations of intellectuals, artists and scholars, the committee went beyond European practices by securing the enthusiastic participation of the stars of new popular arts such as cinema. For the first time, silent-film stars such as Mary Pickford, Douglas Fairbanks Jr and Charlie Chaplin addressed immense crowds to encourage them to enlist or buy Treasury bonds.

In fact, the question of whether or not to become involved in the conflict – like that of how to organize the war effort once the country was involved – were matters of intense debate in the United States. A century on, the relevance of these debates continues to strike the contemporary observer. The proper role of the federal state in organizing the economic and social spheres thus became a burning question. It was at this time that the first, as yet provisional steps were taken towards the interventionist policy that would twenty years later become Franklin Delano Roosevelt's New Deal.

Above all, this would oblige American society as a whole to consider the role of the United States in the world and the conflicts it would have to face. It would also call into question the country's very nature, requiring it to define relations between its original, white Protestant settlers and the immigrants who began arriving in the mid-nineteenth century. In both cases, the debate was intense and has obviously yet to be exhausted.

In this critical moment of the war, however, it was mainly the French and British armies that absorbed and finally repelled the desperate and ferocious onslaught of the Kaiser's armies at the time of Germany's last major offensive in the spring of 1918. The few hundred thousand troops who had arrived in Europe by this time were nearly all still in training in Great Britain or France, either behind the lines or along quiet stretches of the front. So urgent had the situation become, however, that Pershing agreed to place his troops at the disposal of the Allied command – that is, of Foch. Elements of the US 1st, 2nd and 3rd Infantry Divisions (and the US Marine regiments attached to them) thus participated in combat from early June 1918. The 2nd, in particular, actively confronted the leading edge of the German advance at Château-Thierry and Belleau Wood, where it faced the army of Prince Rupprecht of Bavaria. The inexperienced soldiers who went into battle there did so with extreme courage and very heavy casualties. They contributed to repelling the last phase of the final German offensive, known in France as the Second Battle of the Marne.

Then, starting in mid-August and for the remaining hundred days of the conflict, American troops were able to carry out a major offensive in the Argonne against the German army. Though it was now in retreat, the latter was nevertheless still very much capable of fighting and would continue to inflict significant casualties on the Allied armies up till the Armistice. The number of American troops killed in action (50,000, with an additional 40,000 dying as a result of illness, mainly Spanish influenza[10]) may seem slight in comparison with the 1.4 million French and 950,000 British dead. When set against the number of troops actually sent into battle and their number of days in combat, however, it is anything but.

From the outset, in fact, American units suffered the same terrible casualty rates as did other Allied armies when the bulk of their forces first entered the conflict (August 1914 for the French and July 1916 for the British). For newly formed armies, it can be difficult to draw lessons from the setbacks suffered by others, even those of their own allies in a given conflict. In September 1918, the first heavy engagements of American troops, poorly prepared and not particularly well led, thus resulted in massive casualties. Over the official duration of the conflict, American troops would chalk up 200 dead per day, as against 900 for the French and 460 for the British. But if one makes the same calculation starting in summer 1918 – the moment when American troops first came under fire in large numbers – one arrives at a figure of 820 dead per day.

As had earlier been the case for the French and British, the first major engagements of American troops in France were thus proportionally the bloodiest. Under the command of leaders whose enthusiasm was only matched by a lack of experience, the American troops paid a heavy price for American military officials' too-slow apprenticeship in modern warfare.

Beginning on 6 June 1918, the US Marines at Belleau Wood would learn this the hard way. There, the American army was to suffer a casualty rate comparable to that inflicted on the same day thirty-six years later, during the Normandy landings. Why? How?

The present book seeks to help answer these questions.

# CHAPTER 1

## BELLEAU WOOD, 6 JUNE 1918, DAWN

It is 03.30, and the men of the 1st Battalion, 3rd Marine Regiment await the first glimmers of dawn to attack Hill 142, a ridge on the western edge of Belleau Wood. An old seignorial hunting preserve, this little forest is located a few kilometres west of Château-Thierry between two little villages in the *département* of Aisne, Torcy and Bouresches. At this juncture of the war, it constitutes the German offensive's farthest point of advance on French soil – and its deepest since 1914. Paris is less than ninety kilometres away.

Launched on 27 May, the third wave of the German spring offensive had taken the French army by surprise due to its location on the Aisne front. Having expected the assault to take place at the junction of British and French troops farther to the north, the French high command had not stationed its best troops in this long-quiet sector of the Aisne. Under the impact of the German assault, they began to retreat, sometimes in disorder. In short order, the Germans had retaken the Chemin des Dames, which the French had conquered with such difficulty in 1917, and from there crossed the river Aisne. By 29 May, they had occupied Soissons, were threatening Reims and – for the first time since 1914 – had reached the Marne. Paris was threatened. As civilians began to flee the city, the government once again considered evacuating to Bordeaux, as it had done in September 1914.

Given the urgency of the situation, in April General Pershing had for the first time agreed temporarily to integrate his available units into the Allied military command.[11] The 1st Infantry Division was already fighting alongside French troops to the north of the new front, at Cantigny. Then training in Lorraine, the 2nd and 3rd Infantry Divisions were thus made available to the Allied command. They immediately set off by forced march, night and day, for Château-Thierry, south-west of Reims.

In the days leading up to this, however, the French soldiers of General Jean Degoutte's Sixth Army had succeeded in slowing their retreat. Clinging to the ground they held outside Château-Thierry with help from units of the US 3rd Infantry Division, they attempted to slow the German advance via defensive operations. Though this handful of local successes prevented the Germans from crossing the Marne, they came at the cost of heavy casualties. They nevertheless allowed the units of the US 2nd Infantry Division, newly arrived from their position behind the Lorraine front, to start deploying to the right of the French Sixth Army.

This temporary respite made it possible to consolidate the Allied defensive positions more deeply so as to check the upcoming German assault once and for all. General Degoutte planned to counter-attack instead. At a 5 June meeting of Allied general staff, Pershing enthusiastically supported Degoutte's plan. For months, Pershing had been waiting for an opportunity to demonstrate to the highly sceptical

Allied generals that, however inexperienced it might be, the American Expeditionary Force (AEF) was a formidable fighting machine. He also knew that the Marine Corps was particularly motivated and wished to demonstrate its skill in combat. For many years, the Marine Corps's autonomous status had been a subject of controversy in what was at the time a very tight-fisted American Congress. As their name suggests, the marines were originally intended as naval troops: loaded onto warships, they operated cannon, boarded enemy ships and sometimes took part in beach-landing operations. Over the course of the nineteenth century, this last role took on greater importance, with operations in Libya (1805), Mexico (1847), the Philippines (1898) and elsewhere.[12] Thanks to its growing role, the Marine Corps gradually grew in autonomy, eventually becoming the de facto third branch of the US military after the army and navy (the US Air Force did not yet exist). Its existence was threatened, however, with many congressmen demanding that it be integrated into the navy or absorbed by the army as a cost-saving measure.

On the evening of 5 June, Pershing thus gave the commander of the US Marine brigade attached to the US 2nd Infantry Division, Brigadier General James C. Harbord, the order to counter-attack the next day alongside the French 167th Infantry Division.[13] The specific mission of the American soldiers was to take control of Belleau Wood. General Harbord had arrived in France as Pershing's chief of staff. Despite having no experience in this role, a month earlier he had received his superior's authorization to take an active command – in the event, that of the 2nd Infantry Division, consisting of one infantry and one US Marine brigade. For General Harbord, preparing the attack was to be his baptism of fire.

From the outset, the American attack was handicapped by Harbord's lack of personal experience of battle command

and the complexities entailed by the resumption of the war of movement.

Late in the afternoon of 5 June, Harbord thus received the order to attack. After nearly a week of constant movement over unfamiliar roads and terrain, his troops were exhausted and famished. Their movement was slowed by the more or less disorderly retreat of French troops and civilians who, as in September 1914, were fleeing ahead of the fighting. This caused logistical problems, particularly in relation to resupply.

All the same, Harbord rapidly threw together a very basic plan of attack. It consisted of two phases: his troops would first take Hill 142, a high point adjacent to Belleau Wood; they would then attack the wood itself and occupy the villages of Torcy and Bouresches, located on the far side of the wood. At 22.25 on the evening of the 5th, he transmitted his plan to Colonel Wendell Cushing Neville, commander of the 5th Marine Regiment, putting him in charge of the operation and ordering him to attack at 03.45 the following morning, or just before dawn.

At 00.35, Neville in turn transmitted the orders to the commanders of the various battalions of his regiment. They thus received them in the middle of the night, barely three hours before the attack was to begin. The troops had still not received their provisions and many had yet to take up their positions, which they struggled to find in this completely unfamiliar sector.

In both quantitative and qualitative terms, the artillery support provided for the attack was minimal. Six batteries of French 75-mm cannon operated by mixed French and American teams were to support the attack. 'So as not to alert the enemy', however, there would be no initial artillery preparation.

According to French military intelligence supplied to the staff of the 2nd Division, in any case the enemy was 'hardly present or not present at all' in the forest and its immediate surroundings. Given the planned schedule of attack, the

American high command did not consider it necessary to conduct reconnaissance operations.

In fact, an elite regiment of Prince Rupprecht of Bavaria's army containing several machine-gun companies had taken up position in the forest, a rectangular area of roughly one by two kilometres. The forest's dense foliage had not been thinned by fighting. It concealed a steep and furrowed floor containing a number of rocky caves – for the forest's defenders, so many natural bunkers. In short, the forest offered ideal defensive terrain over which the Germans, aware that their advance was slowing, established an in-depth defensive position equipped with a series of machine-gun nests. These were positioned in such a way as to ensure that each machine gun could cover two others with its crossfire.

General Harbord thus distributed roles to his various units stationed around the little village of Lucy-le-Bocage outside Belleau Wood. The job of attacking Hill 142 was given to the 1st Battalion of the 5th Marine Regiment. Just before launching the attack, the battalion commander, one Colonel Terrill, was confronted with the following problem: he was unable to locate two of the four companies under his orders and was thus unable to give them the order to attack. Relying upon inadequately detailed maps drawn up in French, the American units had been on the move for three days without stop. No one had had time to set up telephone communications. Couriers thus set off to comb the surrounding area for the missing companies.

Assuming that the missing units would ultimately turn up, Terrill decided to launch the attack with just half of his troops. The machine-gun company meant to support the advancing infantrymen was also nowhere to be found.

The marines attacked at the break of dawn – at 03.45, to be precise. The American soldiers advanced as they had been taught to do while training in France: in line and divided between four successive waves. They marched in step with bayonets fixed, their bodies upright.

The battalion's formation – several successive lines separated by regular intervals – was inspired by the French tactical manual. It reflected a desire to maintain troop cohesion as far as possible as soldiers advanced under fire, especially when they were inexperienced. An additional advantage of this formation was that a soldier who has to concentrate on the pace of his officer's step and keep a certain distance from his comrades has less time to think about the fact that someone is shooting at him.

Spared the fighting since the summer of 1914, the Belleau Wood zone had not been affected by the war's bombardments and various depredations. Alternating with copses in full leaf, wheat fields (soon to be trod under foot) already stood tall at the foot of Hill 142 on this June day. It was over open ground, however, that the US Marines began their advance.

The first fifty metres were relatively harmless. In his memoirs, one Captain Thompson mentions a sergeant under his command advancing while chewing on the contents of a tin of tuna he had just opened with his bayonet. Another soldier – a corporal – bent down to pick a scarlet-red poppy, which he neatly fastened to his helmet.[14]

Unfortunately for them, the copses and fields of tall wheat efficiently concealed the German machine-gun nests at the forest's edge. Given the progress made in armaments since the middle of the nineteenth century, however, particularly in what concerned the concentration of fire and the extension of its range, it was now impossible to attack entrenched positions over open ground, no matter how disciplined or spirited the assailants. Like the French soldiers of August 1914 in their madder-coloured trousers, the US Marines were thus about to be brutally initiated into the reality of modern weaponry in all its deadliness.

Once the Americans had advanced fifty metres and the lines of their four successive waves were perfectly visible, the Germans opened fire with their machine guns. Many of those in the American first wave collapsed; the rest threw themselves face down on the ground, where they were quickly joined by the men of the second, third and fourth waves. After a moment of hesitation and spurred on by those of their officers and NCOs who were as yet unscathed, the American soldiers resumed their advance, walking or, more often, crawling forward as casualties mounted. In this way they advanced to within fifteen metres of the first German machine-gun nests. They then stood up and, making use of their bayonets, knives and rifle butts, threw themselves into hand-to-hand combat. In little time, the German defenders who had not surrendered or fled to the rear had been killed. The marines then resumed their march – or, rather, crawl – to the next machine-gun nest.

This sequence was repeated up and down the American line and ever deeper within the German positions. Paradoxically and despite the casualties it entailed, the tactic of frontally charging the machine-gun nests doubtless proved more effective than remaining prone under the unremitting fire. One had to have the courage to do so, of course, and all of the troops had to follow, with none remaining on the ground or attempting to retreat. Spurred on by their officers or, failing that, their NCOs and despite their lack of experience, the Marines gave proof of the bravery and aggressiveness for which the corps had traditionally trained them.

They thus ultimately reached their objective, the crest of Hill 142. A small group of them led by a simple corporal even continued beyond the objective and started down the opposite slope. Not meeting any resistance, they pursued their forward momentum until they reached the village of Torcy below.

There, they came upon the German troops, who were already preparing for immediate counter-attack in keeping with their military doctrine. After having sent back one of their number to warn of this imminent counter-attack attack, they dug in at the entrance to the village and were killed on the spot.

On the crest of the hill, the battalion's sole surviving officer, Captain George W. Hamilton, attempted to prepare his troops for the coming attack. Nine of the ten lieutenants under his orders had already been killed. Most platoons had been reduced to a few men under the command of a corporal or sometimes a sergeant. They hastily dug shallow trenches and got into firing position.

Preceded by a short artillery barrage, the German counter-attack then began. In keeping with the latest tactical methods, the German troops advanced in small infiltration groups rather than attacking in line formation. Due to the difficulty of distinguishing friend from foe, the German soldiers advanced slowly. The result was a multitude of individual engagements in which small groups of men fired at one another at close range, threw grenades and ultimately killed one another with knives in hand-to-hand combat. The US Marines once again proved more aggressive than their adversaries in this type of action, and rapidly repelled the attackers, who fled in the direction of Torcy.

It was nearly five in the morning on 6 June when the out-of-contact 1st Battalion companies that had failed to participate in the initial attack began to appear at the foot of the hill.

They were met with relief by Captain Hamilton, whose troops had been decimated. His exhausted US Marines, many of them wounded, were holding precarious positions. He sent one message after another to his superior, Colonel Terrill, begging for reinforcements as well as medics, water and (above all) ammunition. For the supplies with which these men had set off in their packs a few hours earlier were nearly exhausted.[15] Hamilton feared they would soon have to face a new German counter-attack and realized that he was isolated on the crest and potentially vulnerable to encirclement: the French regiment that was supposed to cover his left flank was far behind, having chosen – rationally enough – not to rush forward into enemy fire. By this stage of the war, French units confronted with dense enemy fire had learned to halt their advance and wait for effective artillery support before once again setting off under its cover. And the US Marine battalion that was supposed to protect his right flank had moved much farther right, completely losing contact with Hamilton's men. Not only had the attack been poorly prepared but, on top of that, there was hardly any coordination among the various units. There were no telephone links and groves of trees prevented visual communication. Foot couriers, finally, had a hard time finding their bearings.

Captain Hamilton's message summarized the situation with sober clarity:

> We are digging trenches and have four machine guns in place. We have been counter-attacked several times but so far have held this hill. Our casualties are very heavy [underscored in the original]. We need medical aid badly, cannot locate any hospital apprentices and need many. We will need artillery assistance to hold this line tonight. Ammunition of all kinds is needed…

> George W. Hamilton

P.S. All my officers are gone.[16]

However, in keeping with what is a relatively commonplace military-bureaucratic practice (and one far from limited to the US army), the alarming news of the situation late that morning only reached the high command in progressively watered down and euphemistic form. Colonel Terrill received Hamilton's frenetic calls for help. Yet in reporting to his superior, Colonel Neville, Terrill did not go into casualties in detail but rather insisted on the fact that the desired objective had been achieved. Neville, in turn, assured General Harbord that the operation had been a complete success, with all objectives achieved, and extrapolated from this fact that casualties had been kept to a minimum.

It was thus in complete good conscience that, despite the already advanced hour, early that afternoon and on the strength of the information reaching him – ever brighter and more reassuring as it travelled up the hierarchy – General Harbord gave the order to begin the second phase of the operation planned for that day: a direct attack on Belleau Wood itself.

# CHAPTER 2

## 6 JUNE 1918, 17.00: THE ATTACK

At US Marine brigade headquarters late that morning, General Harbord took stock of that day's fighting on Hill 142. The resulting analysis was very optimistic: the desired objective had been achieved, and that was all that counted. It was reported to him that, despite their lack of experience, the marines had shown the courage and aggressiveness expected of them and this was entirely true.

Casualties thus mattered little (though it was impossible to get a clear view of them at this point, it is true). Nor did it much matter that the US Marines' situation was so worrisome faced with the prospect of a new German counter-attack – the few who remained were exhausted, hungry, thirsty, short on equipment and ammunition and surrounded by the wounded, the dying and the dead. Harbord seems to have believed that events had justified that morning's choice of tactic: a head-on assault without any particular preparation, reconnaissance (neither of the terrain nor of enemy positions) or real preliminary bombardment. He thus prepared to do it all over again late that afternoon, sending a larger number of troops against a more ambitious and even better defended objective: Belleau Wood.

In the early afternoon, he thus sent the following instructions to the various units under his orders: the 3rd Battalion of the 5th Marine Regiment, led by Major Dan Berry, was to attack the western part of the wood. The 3rd Battalion of the 6th Marine Regiment, led by Major Barton Sibley, was to attack the eastern part. On the eastern side of Sibley's men, the 2nd Battalion of the 6th Marine Regiment was to advance towards the village of Bouresches. The entire operation was placed under the authority of Colonel Albertus Catlin, commander of the 6th Marine Regiment.

The question of whether or not the battalion from the 5th Marine Regiment was to report to the commander of the 6th was never clarified, a fact that would have consequences for the various units' ability to communicate with one another in order to coordinate their movements.

This summarizes the essential points of the operational plan prepared by General Harbord and his general staff. There was to be no preliminary artillery barrage because, as he would later write, 'it was a surprise operation'. And no preliminary reconnaissance to determine German positions or troop strength in the wood. Harbord relied upon the forty-eight-hour-old reports of French military intelligence, which described German troops as either minimally present or totally absent from Belleau Wood.

At the regimental level, much more worrisome information had begun to make its way back from the field. Several reconnaissance operations had been carried out in the wood by small groups of American soldiers, often on their own initiative. They returned with descriptions of a terrain sprinkled with machine-gun nests placed so as to cover one another; this was the case across the entire depth of the wood.

For, in reality, the Germans had entered Belleau Wood on 2 June, the day of their farthermost advance. They had immediately recognized the forest as offering a perfect defensive position: in addition to the cover provided by the dense foliage of the trees, the terrain was sprinkled with boulders and criss-crossed by ravines, offering a choice of particularly well-protected firing positions. Altogether, the Germans installed more than fifteen heavy and 200 light machine guns in the forest. As we have seen, each position was generally covered by two others. All of this was held by around 1,200 men from the 461st Regiment of the German 237th Infantry Division. At this stage of the war, these men were of course suffering under the strain of an offensive that had begun more than a month earlier, as well as from supply problems and the effects of the onset of the Spanish flu. But they were experienced, disciplined and still ready to fight.

In a way that only rendered frontal assault yet more difficult, if that were possible, the US Marines' starting positions outside the village of Lucy-le-Bocage were more than 400 metres from the first clumps of trees of Belleau Wood, which faced it. The marines had to cross this distance almost without cover and in full view of the German machine guns that lay in wait for them at the forest's edge.

Around 16.30, the American artillery began to fire aimlessly on Belleau Wood, causing little damage. By contrast, the German's return fire concentrated on Lucy-le-Bocage, the zone where the marines had assembled in hastily dug trenches as they waited to attack.

It was then that famous *Chicago Tribune* reporter Floyd Gibbons arrived on the scene. The American press of the time had reached its largest ever audience and was nearly the public's only source of information for local and international events. The Wilson administration was very much aware of its influence and went out of its way to facilitate access to the field of operations for 'patriot' journalists. Within the armed forces themselves, the Marine Corps showed particular concern for its image. Its popularity in the eyes of public opinion enhanced the quality of its recruits and above all encouraged members of Congress to support its specific budgetary subsidies. Gibbons thus presented himself to Colonel Neville, from whom he requested – and obtained – authorization to head directly for the 4th Marine Regiment's starting trenches.

Here is a passage from his account of the attack:

> It was a beautiful sight […] The platoons started in good order and advanced steadily into the field between clumps of woods. It was flat country with no protection of any sort except the bending wheat. The enemy opened up at once and it seemed […] as if the air was full of red-hot nails. The losses were terrific.[17]

The Americans' advance thus began to slow and, as a growing number of soldiers fell to the ground – killed, wounded or simply anxious to protect themselves – the neat and orderly attacking lines collapsed.

At this point in Floyd Gibbons's account there took place an episode that would be recounted multiple times in the American press and subsequently included in Marine Corps hagiographies: 'As the lines of attack crumbled, the voice of a sergeant rang out in the chaos: "Come on, you sons of bitches! Do you want to live for ever?"'[18] In his report, Gibbons himself drew a connection with Victor Hugo's account of the Battle of Waterloo and the French general Pierre Cambronne's one-word reply to the British general Sir Charles Colville on being called to surrender: "*Merde!*" With a fondness for short and snappy turns of phrase, the American press of the time recounted the incident innumerable times in order to underscore the invincible spirit of the 'doughboys' in general and the US Marines in particular. Gibbons's account of this day for its part breaks off shortly thereafter, as the journalist was seriously wounded in the face several minutes later.[19]

Be that as it may, the marines continued to advance in overlapping waves and soon succeeded in reaching the edge of the wood, which they then entered. There, the environment almost instantaneously changed for the attackers. The relief, the tree density, the sudden darkness and above all the intensity of machine-gun fire combined constantly to break up the marines' formation. The time for advancing in lines by battalions was over. Depending on natural obstacles and, above all, the growing number of dead and wounded, groups of attackers that had begun as companies gradually became platoons and then sections as they advanced. Soon, they were just small groups of men moving forward over the narrow, sloping paths under the authority of the highest-ranking or most enterprising among them, each group advancing at its own pace depending on the relief and, above all, the enemy machine-gun fire. Some groups found themselves pinned down as soon as they entered the wood; others, by contrast, made their way in between the various German positions more or less without mishap. There was thus almost no contact between the groups that had entered the wood. Within a given unit, as-yet-unscathed officers were unable to locate the position of their comrades and particularly of their leaders. Judging by the noise of machine-gun fire, they attempted to locate the scene of fighting. In the growing darkness and din of battle, they sought to determine whether they had fallen behind their advancing comrades or had rather moved ahead of them. Soldiers who found themselves cut off from their units, by contrast, individually attached themselves to the little groups now scattered like a leopard's spots throughout the wood. Dusk would soon come and, with it, darkness.

By nightfall, some US Marine units had thus reached their initial objectives: the villages of Torcy and Bouresches, respectively located at the north- and south-western foot of Belleau Wood. Inside the wood itself, however, a tangled patchwork of German and American positions prevailed. The time had come to dig in for the night and prepare for nocturnal attack and counter-attack.

A swarm of runners of differing speeds raced down the hill towards Lucy-le-Bocage, all carrying nearly identical messages: we desperately need stretcher-bearers, water, entrenching tools and above all – above all! – ammunition.

In just a few hours of fighting, more than 220 US Marines had been killed and more than a thousand wounded.[20] It was the bloodiest day of fighting in the history of the US Marines, tallying more losses than the corps had suffered since its creation in 1775 – and so it would remain until the first day of battle for the Pacific island of Tarawa in November 1943.

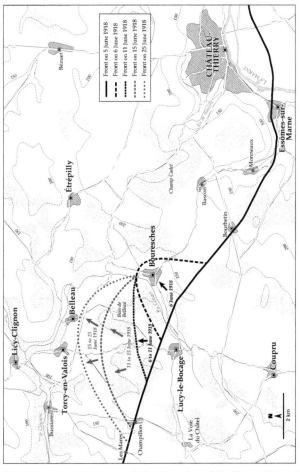

*The Various Stages of the Battle of Belleau Wood*

# CHAPTER 3

## THE BATTLE OF BELLEAU WOOD RAGES ON

The tactical choices made by the Americans and Germans in pursuing the fighting could not have differed more. As day broke on 7 June, the situation in Belleau Wood was confused. Small groups of marines had dug in around a number of German positions spread throughout the wood. As the hours passed, these groups grew larger as men who had found themselves cut off during the attack joined up with them. The better part of the wood was nevertheless still occupied by the Germans.

General Harbord and the American command began at this time to get a somewhat clearer picture of the battlefield, thanks to the foot messengers constantly coming and going to beg for medical care, provisions and ammunition. It thus appeared that, contrary to the general staff's first impressions, the disorganized and bloody attack of the previous day had been far from decisive. Although a number of marines had succeeded in pushing on to the villages of Torcy (before retreating) and Bouresches (successfully), each of which anchored one flank of the battlefield, the wood itself was far from being under American control.

The day before, however, Harbord had announced a decisive success to the general staff of the 2nd Division on the basis of the fragmentary, incomplete and distorted reports that had made their way to him. The very conscientious press liaison service had immediately announced this news to the correspondents of the American press. The next morning, newspaper headlines across the United States thus heralded the marines' triumph. Since the United States' entry into the war more than a year earlier, the lack of major battles involving American troops had starved the country's newspapers of stories of decisive American victories. Belleau Wood was thus an opportunity to make up for this.

But now it was necessary to make sure that reality more closely coincided with the newspapers' headlines. There was thus to be a fresh attack, this time to really take control of the wood. Before doing so, however, it was necessary over the course of 7 June to consolidate the American positions into a series of nearly continuous lines, rescue wounded soldiers who had been cut off from their comrades and supply the men with food, water and ammunition. The attack would thus not be resumed until the morning of the 8th.

In retrospect, the German troops' occupation of Belleau Wood represented one of their farthest points of advance in June 1918. Farther west, outside Château-Thierry, their progress had already been halted on 2 June by units of the US 3rd Infantry Division (among others). On the morning of the 7th, however, the French authorities, who assumed that the Germans would pursue their advance at any cost, nevertheless continued to prepare for the capital's defence and the evacuation of essential services.

Somewhat more surprisingly, the Germans were for their part also preparing to counter-attack. Immediately counter-attacking to retake a position was of course a mainstay of German doctrine. In the present instance, however, committing additional men and materiel to defend or retake Belleau Wood seemed at odds with pursuing an offensive that had enjoyed some success since being launched a few days earlier. Bypassing local points of resistance such as this one in order to pursue retreating French troops, to deny them time to regroup around solid defensive positions and, above all, potentially to open the way to Paris for the first time since September 1914 might seem more important objectives.

The Germans' decision to challenge the Americans for possession of a wooded hill of limited strategic interest and covering an area of no more than one by two kilometres may thus seem surprising.

The German general staff nevertheless decided to send fresh troops to the area in reinforcement. Two elite divisions, the Prussian 5th Guards Division and the 28th Infantry Division, were withdrawn from their position outside Noyon, where the next German offensive was to take place, and sent to face the Americans in the south-east.

For the German generals attached great importance to the relative performance of the American army in both psychological and materiel terms. Ever since the Americans had entered the war, the German general staff had issued very critical public and internal assessments of US military potential on the Western Front. The tenor of their comments was more or less as follows: 'American soldiers are totally inexperienced and their officers are disorganized and undisciplined. They will see that hunting down Sioux or Mexican bandits and confronting the German army are two very different things.'

Over the course of the preceding days, however, the various American units engaged in the fighting (the US 1st Division at Cantigny on 28 May, the 3rd Division at

Château-Thierry and the 2nd Division at Belleau Wood) had demonstrated real fighting spirit and, despite high casualties, convincing results.

Ludendorff himself was concerned about the propaganda effect these first American successes would have on the Allies and their impact on German troop morale. On 8 June, he thus generally instructed the commanders of his army to attack immediately and in strength any American units that appeared on the front, 'so as to impede the formation of an American army'.[21]

A report from the commander of the German 28th Infantry Division, General von Bohn, very clearly laid out the overall stakes of the battle then underway in this relatively isolated little wood:

If the Americans take the advantage on the Western Front, even if for only a short while, it will have disastrous consequences for the morale of the Alliance and the future course of the war. The battle ahead is not merely for the control of this or that otherwise unimportant village or wood. Rather, it is to determine whether the Anglo-American publicity machine will succeed in presenting the American army as of equal or even greater worth than the German army.

Having become more of a symbolic than tactical issue for both sides, there would thus be intense fighting for control of Belleau Wood.

The US Marines' attack on the morning of 8 June was a total failure. The previous day had been spent trying to consolidate their scattered positions inside the wood by forming several continuous lines. This was not done without losses, with each movement of a unit or small group of men seeming to run up against an unexpected German position or machine-gun nest.

And yet all had to be supplied with water, food and ammunition under more or less constant German fire. Attempts also had to be made to locate, treat and evacuate the wounded – an exhausting task on a battlefield – all while under enemy bombardment. For the time being, in fact, the bodies of American and German soldiers were left where they fell. During the day, the marines repelled two German counter-attacks from Torcy.

At dawn on 8 June, while many of his men were still gnawing on their cold rations, Harbord gave a new order to attack with the intention of securing the southern part of the wood. As before, he dispensed with any artillery preparation.

The result was predictable: as soon as they began to move forward, the marines were mowed down by the German machine guns' crossfire and quickly forced to halt their advance. The surviving officers passed on the message that their men, exhausted after two days of fighting, appeared no longer capable of advancing under such dense fire. After finally launching an artillery barrage to cover their retreat, Harbord called his men back in early afternoon.

For his part, on 9 June Ludendorff launched a new offensive between Noyon and Montdidier, north-east of Château-Thierry. It is from here that the two elite divisions sent to Belleau Wood had been withdrawn; they thus did not take part in the German attack. In the course of the first two days, the Germans succeeded in advancing around ten kilometres. Beginning on 11 June, however, French counter-attacks halted the German advance and began to recapture lost ground, taking many prisoners along the way.

That same day, reinforcements, materiel and supplies once

again began to shuttle back and forth to Belleau Wood under nearly continuous German bombardment.

The next attack – on 10 June – would also end in failure for the Americans. This time, General Harbord decided to launch a massive artillery bombardment on the eve of his men's attack, which was set to begin at 04.30. His troops were to be preceded by a rolling barrage that was meant to move forward as they advanced over the terrain. The marines did indeed advance in the first hours of fighting that morning, and optimistic and satisfied reports continued to reach Harbord until midday. As was his habit, the general did not fail to report that it had been a dazzling success to his direct superior at 2nd Division headquarters, General Omar Bundy.

The constant bombardment bred confusion, however, and the hilly terrain over which the fighting took place made it difficult to get one's bearings. Alas for the marines, their actual advance fell well short of that reported by their officers. Inexperienced and disoriented, they were reliant upon their sketchy and imperfect maps. Though they believed they had more or less achieved their local objectives, they had in reality only just returned to the point their comrades had reached two days earlier before being forced to withdraw. They were in fact at least 800 metres short of their objectives.

The American artillerymen, what's more, demonstrated their relative inexperience at this stage of the war. For one thing, their fire was often short or inaccurate, frequently raining down on their own troops, whose positions were not known to the artillerymen. Their barrage fire was also of little effect against the still-dense forest, with detonators improperly timed on many shells. Most of the shells thus exploded high in the air after coming into contact with the treetops, causing little damage to the well-dug and entrenched machine-gun nests below. These, meanwhile, wreaked havoc upon the attackers.

The result was that, between 1 June, when the first units began to arrive, and 10 June, the US 2nd Infantry Division lost nearly 10,000 men, killed and wounded, including more than 200 officers. Of this total, over 5,000 were US Marines, more than 120 of whom were officers.[22]

On 11 June, the marines attacked again, ultimately with the same disastrous results. In late afternoon, Harbord finally became aware of the fact that his marines were far from controlling Belleau Wood. He thus ordered the commander of the 2nd Battalion 5th Marine Regiment, Colonel Frederic M. Wise, to attack at dawn the next morning and take control of the northern part of the wood. At 04.30, the US Marines thus once again recklessly threw themselves into battle. Alas, the officers – inexperienced, unfamiliar with the terrain over which they were fighting, equipped with totally inadequate maps and, like their men, exhausted after several days of nearly incessant combat – found themselves totally disoriented in the wood. While the American soldiers fought with real drive and captured a number of machine-gun nests, most often in hand-to-hand fighting, they lost their bearings and, instead of advancing northwards, headed south with heavy losses.

Late in the day, Colonel Wise was nevertheless persuaded that his men had reached most of their objectives. He made this known to Harbord, who once again immediately sent the good news back to divisional general staff, where the press liaison service showed the same alacrity as before in sharing the news with newspaper correspondents. Throughout the day, Wise continued to believe that he held the northern part of Belleau Wood despite the growing doubts of his subordinates. These sent out reconnaissance patrols, which confirmed the sad reality: the northern portion of the wood – the objective of that day's bloody attack – was still almost entirely under German control. That did not prevent the *New York Times* on 12 June from once again devoting its front page to news of the marines' final conquest of Belleau Wood.[23]

The 12 June attack would, for its part, be a partial success. That morning, Harbord once again ordered Wise to attack and this time to do his best to achieve the planned objective. The 2nd Battalion thus attacked in late afternoon, once again behind an artillery barrage. But as the American commander's reports continued to overestimate the progress made the day before, the shells fell far behind the German defenders directly facing the Americans. Despite everything, the American troops ultimately succeeded in advancing, penetrating several lines of German defences as they did so.

But with night falling and Wise's men exhausted, he was obliged to inform Harbord that he had only around 300 able-bodied men left. Despite some individual reinforcements received while the fighting was still going on, this figure suggests a casualty rate of over 70 per cent. Wise rightly concluded that his men had pushed themselves to their limit and that no more could be asked of them. But just as Harbord was getting ready to relieve his front-line troops, intelligence gathered from the interrogation of prisoners indicated an imminent German counter-attack. The Germans' constantly intensifying bombardment of the American positions seemed to confirm this.

The German counter-attacks of 13 and 14 June were by contrast turned back with heavy losses for the attackers. Two days of intense German bombardment, including gas attacks, forced the marines to spend long periods wearing the very uncomfortable gas masks with which they were equipped. At the same time, the German infantry carried out several attacks against the village of Bouresches at the wood's edge, which had been taken on 6 June. But the marines were reinforced by an infantry regiment (the 23rd) in time to repel all of these attacks. Casualties were high on both sides. The German 237th Infantry Regiment, for example, which had consisted of 3,200 soldiers on 4 June, was down to 1,500 able-bodied men by that evening.

Though it did not last long, the US Marines welcomed their partial and temporary relief in mid-June. Aware that his troops were exhausted after having hardly slept or eaten a hot meal in more than a week, on the evening of the 14th Harbord began to organize the relief, one battalion at a time, of the two US Marine regiments (the 5th and 6th) that comprised his brigade. However, given the optimistic (and erroneous) reports he had sent over the preceding days to the general staffs of the US 2nd Division and the French Fourth Army, to which it was attached, it was some time before his requests for reinforcement were granted (since it was believed that the wood had already been more or less conquered). It was ultimately only on the 15th that units of the US Third Army (in particular, the 7th Infantry Regiment) began to arrive from Château-Thierry to relieve the exhausted marines. Harbord profited from the brief respite during which the units were relieved (and which the Germans used to reinforce the defensive positions they continued to hold in the northern part of the wood) to restructure his command. Reproaching Colonel Wise for having been mistaken – and for having misled him – as to the position of his forces inside the wood, he dismissed him from the command of his battalion.

With German resistance beginning to weaken, the American forces launched successive attacks over the course of the last days of June. On 20 June, Harbord sent the fresh but inexperienced troops of the 7th Infantry Regiment into battle. In the interval, the Germans had had the time to reinforce their defences, and the American infantry regiment lost 300 men over the course of the day. A new attack the next day had the same result. Harbord had no choice but to recall the marine units that had had a few days to rest and were now somewhat familiar with the terrain. Late in the afternoon of 23 June, the marines once again attacked without artillery preparation, though this time mortar and machine-gun fire covered their advance. They hardly gained 200 metres and once again suffered heavy casualties – roughly 130 men.

On the 24th, a meeting of senior officers was held at the headquarters of the 2nd Division's commander, General Bundy. This time, it was decided to carry out a one-day bombardment of the German positions with the support of French artillery. Eighteen batteries were put in place and fired continuously for fourteen hours. At 17.00 hours on the 25th, the marines once again attacked the wood's north-western fringe. This time, German resistance began to weaken, particularly as a result of the bombardment. That night, many Germans began to leave the wood in little groups and head north. Others surrendered.

At dawn on 26 June, the marines finally reached the northern edge of the wood, in the process capturing thirty machine guns and 300 German prisoners, but losing another 150 men. In the morning, the commander of the 2nd Division, General Bundy, received the following message: 'The entirety of Belleau Wood is now in the hands of the marines.'

And this time it was true.

With the passage of time, one may legitimately wonder: what was the true tactical and psychological impact of the Battle of Belleau Wood?

On 30 June, General Degoutte, commander of the French Sixth Army, to which the American 2nd Division was attached, published the following order:

> Given the brilliant conduct of the 4th Brigade of the American 2nd Division, which, in a determined attack, took the village of Bouresches and Belleau Wood, resolutely defended by a large enemy force, the general commanding the Sixth Army orders that, henceforth, Belleau Wood now be called 'Marine Brigade Wood' in all official correspondence.

Belleau Wood is today seen as an important episode in the history of the Marine Corps and is a source of pride. From the outset, however, this action has been a matter of controversy within the US Army. General Pershing's general staff even (unsuccessfully) intervened to have General Degoutte's order rescinded. Pershing himself was very unhappy that political and media attention focused almost exclusively on the Marine Corps, with hardly any mention made of the army units that participated in the fighting. The controversy subsequently spread to the significance of the battle itself.

At one extreme, some claimed that the US Marines had quite simply won the war by stopping the German army at Belleau Wood, thereby depriving it of the possibility of breaking through towards Paris. For others, it was a senseless engagement that was poorly led by commanding officers and in which heavy casualties were incurred in pursuit of an objective of no real strategic importance.

With the invaluable benefit of historical hindsight, a more nuanced and less extreme analysis seems possible.

In the very first days of June, the situation was indeed perilous for the French army. Surprised by a German attack in a place where none was expected, some French troops retreated more or less in disorder. The French command hesitated to bring in reinforcements from the northern sector as that was where it expected a German attack, which was in fact launched on the 9th. The arrival of the US 2nd and 3rd Divisions from Metz relieved it of the need to carry out such a transfer. In early June, the US 3rd Division outside Château-Thierry thus greatly contributed to slowing and then repelling the German advance on the Marne. By covering the French retreat and preventing it from turning into a rout, the 2nd Division's arrival outside Belleau Wood for its part allowed the situation to be stabilized.

What presents a problem for *ex post facto* analysis is primarily the decision to attack Belleau Wood immediately at dawn on the day following the marines' arrival, particularly as this did not allow the men to recuperate or reconnoitre the terrain, and took place in the absence of artillery preparation. This decision had in fact been taken by General Degoutte, commander of the French Sixth Army. It was nevertheless accepted with enthusiasm by a portion of the American military command – first and foremost Pershing himself, who was keen to demonstrate the training and military prowess of his troops to allies whose ill-concealed disdain rankled him.

A second surprise for the historian: the German commander's decision to cling to the terrain after 6 June and ferociously defend the wood, going so far as to transfer for that purpose units that had been allocated to the upcoming offensive. This reflected a determination on the part of the German general staff, starting with Ludendorff, to establish emphatically the German army's individual, materiel and tactical superiority over its American counterpart, whose troops had just begun to arrive on the battlefields in large numbers.

In fact, the US Army at this time was an explosive mixture. Going into battle for the first time in particularly difficult circumstances, its highly motivated troops were hampered by the tactical deficiencies of its command structure (lack of reconnaissance, logistical failings, non-existent communications, absent or insufficient artillery cover, and so on).

The behaviour of the US Marines as they charged the machine-gun nests in a way resembled that of the French soldiers of August 1914, who had also been called upon to charge the enemy over open ground, bayonets fixed. It must also be kept in mind that, following a long and bloody apprenticeship (for their troops), the French officer corps only began to acquire the techniques of combined infantry and artillery manoeuvre long after summer 1914.[24] One is here confronted with the nearly unavoidable learning curve of modern war, deadly and incompressible for its actors and victims alike. Belleau Wood shows that it continued to be challenging for one army to transmit this 'learning curve' to another, even when they were allies. French instructors could of course rapidly train the rank-and-file American soldier in how to use a Chauchat light machine gun, gas-mask protocol or how to advance as a group in four, regularly spaced lines. Far more difficult was training their officers, subaltern and senior alike, in the tactical lessons of trench warfare and the war of materiel. Apart from the question of time, the US general staff would have had to support much more vigorously this process of 'updating' its officer corps, the vast majority of whom had no prior military experience. This was not support Pershing wished to give.

Yet, by accepting, day after day, high casualties in pursuit of a dubious strategic objective, the marines made it clear to their adversaries, from Ludendorff to the rank-and-file machine-gunner crouching behind his boulder, that the American soldier was an obviously determined – and thus formidable – adversary. And millions more were on their way...

While it is clear from this point of view that the marines did not really save Paris in June 1918, they did contribute to tipping the conflict in the Allies' favour by discouraging their enemies. And yet, had circumstances been ever so slightly different, their sacrifice at the gates of the Paris Basin might never have been.

# CHAPTER 4

## EARLY 1917: THE STATE OF THE CONFLICT ON THE EVE OF THE UNITED STATES' ENTRY INTO THE WAR

In January 1917, the war was well into its third year, something that none of the belligerents' general staffs had anticipated in August 1914. Worse yet, the conflict seemed both to intensify and to expand over time. New countries (Italy, Romania, Portugal, and so on) became involved. New battlefields appeared on the map (in the Balkans and the Middle East, for example). Millions of men continued to be killed.

On the Western Front, 1916 was marked by the titanic battles of Verdun and the Somme. But neither the German offensive in February nor the Franco-British one in July achieved its objective: breaking through the enemy front and resuming the war of movement of the conflict's earliest days. But the casualties mounted (dead, wounded and prisoners), putting ever greater pressure on the belligerents' dwindling demographic reserves. They had little choice but to recruit ever younger and older cohorts of men as well as those in poor (mental or physical) health.

On the Eastern Front, 1916 witnessed tsarist Russia's last major military initiative, the Brusilov offensive. Originally planned to coincide with the Anglo-French offensive on the Somme and relieve the Italian army against the Austro-Hungarians, it at first enjoyed some success. By coming to the rescue of its ally, the German army was able to stop the Russian offensive and, in doing so, fatally undermine the tsarist regime – a setback the latter, weakened by internal contradictions, would not survive. At the same time and despite German support, the Austrian army never truly recovered from its losses and, in summer 1918, collapsed.

On the peripheral fronts, the tide of war hesitated to turn decisively in favour of one camp or the other.

Since August 1915, Italy had been at war with its former Austro-Hungarian allies from the Triple Alliance. Faced with mainly Austrian troops, the conflict quickly became bogged down in the Alpine massifs. An Italian expeditionary corps also participated in the conflict in Albania, a land towards which Italy harboured strong colonial ambitions.

In the Balkans, the conflict expanded in August 1916 with Romania's entry into the war against Austro-Hungary and its immediate invasion by Bulgaria. Mainly relying on French troops, the Allies established a new front in the Balkans from their base in Thessaloníki (which was at the time theoretically neutral Greek territory). There, they faced off against a determined enemy – typhus – the devastating effects of which immobilized vast numbers of troops.

In the Middle East, 1916 saw the Ottoman Empire – which a year earlier had successfully repelled the Anglo-French attack on the Dardanelles – relentlessly lose ground to the

Arab Revolt led by Hashemite Prince Faisal of Arabia and supported by the British.[25]

The conflict's globalization and the technological strides made by the belligerents tended to accelerate the tactical transformation of their armies. First and foremost, this occurred at the industrial level: 1916 witnessed the advent of what the Germans called *Materialschlacht*, or a 'war of materiel'. In addition to troops, the ability to produce, obtain and move considerable quantities of materiel to the front (munitions, artillery and, soon, tanks and aeroplanes) became absolutely decisive if one hoped to win.

The demography of European societies also became an essential aspect of the conflict. Together with the offensives of 1916, the very duration of hostilities contributed to exhausting gradually the reservoir of young men – and, soon, less young and very young men – available to take part in the fighting. Starting in 1916, countries like Great Britain, which had until then relied on volunteers to supply their armies with men, had to resort to conscription. In addition to soldiers, road workers, miners, dockworkers, and so on were also needed. Countries like France that had already resorted to conscription found themselves obliged to recruit massive numbers of foreign workers from their colonies or elsewhere. This explains the arrival of many South East Asian and Chinese workers in France.

In any case, in what was now a global conflict, the ability to move men, raw materials and equipment of all kinds over long distances – in particular, oceans – became absolutely critical.

It was precisely in this domain that, in early 1917, Imperial Germany took what would be a fateful initiative: the resumption of unrestricted submarine warfare, a move that was ultimately to drag the United States into the conflict.

# CHAPTER 5

## WHY DIDN'T THE UNITED STATES ENTER THE WAR IN AUGUST 1914?

Although American public opinion in August 1914 largely sympathized with France, Britain and above all recently invaded Belgium, there was a broad consensus against directly participating in this conflict between European nations.

In the British Empire's former (white) colonies, by contrast, Britain's entry into the war had immediately provoked a considerable outpouring of solidarity. Canada, Australia, New Zealand, South Africa, Newfoundland, Labrador and Bermuda enthusiastically entered the conflict and from the outset decided to send troops to fight in Europe. Though these dominions were now only under the very nominal authority of the British sovereign, they remained very keenly attached to the mother country. In August 1914, the first volunteer contingents from the dominions were formed.[26]

There was nothing comparable in the United States, which had only gained its independence from the United Kingdom after a long conflict. The last military episode of this conflict – the bombardment and burning of Washington DC by the Royal Navy in 1812 – had taken place just a century earlier. Relations with the United Kingdom had of course markedly improved since then. In the late nineteenth century and on both sides of the Atlantic, many spoke proudly of a shared, enterprising and masterful 'Anglo-Saxon race', in keeping with the very widespread Western racial discourse of the time. In the final years of the nineteenth century, what's more, immigration to the United States had markedly accelerated. But now the vast majority of new arrivals no longer originated in the British Isles or the broader Anglo-Saxon world, but rather in central, Eastern and southern Europe.

These recent arrivals were looking for a new beginning and better economic opportunities. Having often been mistreated in Europe, they valued a political environment that was at least in theory respectful of individual liberties. It would be tempting to say in retrospect that they were united by a conviction: that their individual fate and that of their families should no longer be exposed to the impact of an event totally beyond their control such as the misfortunes of an Austrian archduke in a Bosnian village...

Equipped with a relatively weak federal state and subject to perpetual social and economic transformation, American society was, if not fractured, at least clearly fragmented along the lines of several criteria. Whether defined by ethnic origin, religious identity, geographical region or, obviously, social position, the various groups of individuals who composed American society profoundly differed in how they looked upon the coming war.

Regarding foreign-policy issues in the United States – and the decision as to whether or not to participate in the first global conflict was indeed such – the various positions were determined by four principal criteria that influenced individual attitudes towards the fighting.

The first was geographical in nature (the industrial north, the Deep South, the agricultural Midwest, the pioneer west): American territory contained relatively different populations. Next was the matter of religion, with the split between various Protestant denominations, Irish and Italian Catholics and, more recently, Jews. There was also the very real fact of racial segregation, which took on a more or less formal character from one state to the next. Finally, there was the fact of social and economic fragmentation, a phenomenon that became increasingly marked with industrial development. It set farmers and ranchers against the growing urban population and, as in Europe, the working classes against merchants and industrialists.

By far the largest and most influential of these groups were the white Anglo-Saxon Protestants, or 'WASPs'. Long settled in the country, they pulled most of the political strings at the federal level. Within this group, Yankees – inhabitants of the urbanized and industrialized north-east – had been behind secession from the British Crown 150 years earlier. Paradoxically, it was in this group that the Anglo-British cause found its strongest supporters. As early as August 1914, former Republican president Theodore Roosevelt – penultimate predecessor in that office of Woodrow Wilson, who was elected in 1912 (and was the first Democrat to reach the White House since the Civil War) – campaigned for the creation under his authority of an American volunteer legion to fight alongside the British and French. Though his efforts came to nothing, a number of volunteers, many of them drawn from prestigious East Coast universities, individually became involved in the conflict, some as early as August 1914. They did so by joining the Canadian army or the French Foreign Legion.[27] Others volunteered to serve in the air force and in 1915 were led to create the 'Lafayette Squadron' in France. Yet others volunteered for non-combatant roles. This was the case, in particular, of those who signed up to drive the ambulances of the American Field Service (AFS), which had been created in Paris on the initiative of American Quakers.[28] A remarkable number of American writers (and future writers) served in this capacity. Among others, they included Ernest Hemingway, John Dos Passos and even Gertrude Stein. Nor was the role of front-line ambulance driver free of danger: of 2,500 volunteer drivers, 127 were killed in action (some after enlisting in the expeditionary corps from the summer of 1917).[29]

It should be noted that the American volunteers were motivated by various considerations that went well beyond simple moral enthusiasm for the Allied cause. As has always and everywhere been the case, some men of all ages find the prospect of combat attractive and fascinating no matter the circumstances. Finally, a few eccentrics overcame difficulties to make their own way to the front.

As an example, it is worth briefly mentioning two American volunteers described by the Swiss poet Blaise Cendrars in his autobiographical account *La Main coupée*, whose title means 'the severed hand'.[30] These two surgeons from Chicago enlisted as ordinary soldiers in the Foreign Legion. The first, Buywater, was seventy-two years old; the second, Wilson, was sixty-eight. (Even more so than today, the Legion sought to avoid discouraging those receptive to its call, even when this call came late in life…) Both were Mennonites, a German-origin congregation that traces its roots to sixteenth-century Anabaptism. The rules governing this congregation allow its members to bear arms but not use them – something that, once again, did not seem to worry the Legion hierarchy particularly. By contrast, one of the sect's articles of faith is to dress in keeping with the customs in force at the time of Christ. To the great displeasure of their sergeants, Buywater and Wilson thus tore off all of the buttons from their uniform and replaced them with improvised laces. But it was the stated reason for their enlistment that most set them apart. As they explained to Cendrars, they were largely indifferent to the quarrels between the French and the Germans. No, what led these doctors to sign up as ordinary soldiers was the prospect of taking frequent baths in the mud of the trenches, from which they expected a very beneficial impact on their health:

> When the time for their guard duty had arrived, they ran to the battlements, undressed, quickly undid themselves (their gear being held together by a system composed of bits of string) and mounted guard naked (their rifles in dust covers), kneeling, revelling in it, rubbing their old skin with both hands, splashing around with delight in the stinking mud, looking at us young ones up and down with scorn.[31]

Alas, the benefit of mudbaths for life expectancy was not to be scientifically demonstrated on this occasion. In 1915, Buywater was killed in an assault on Vimy Ridge; Wilson died in the fighting for Souchez cemetery.

In the south of the United States, the memory of Britain's hostile stance towards the Confederacy during the Civil War played a role. As in the west, the population above all lived from farming and ranching and was weary of any profit that might be made by northern industrialists from the country's involvement in the war in Europe.

During the second half of the nineteenth century, many immigrants arriving in the United States from Germany and the Scandinavian countries established themselves in the country's Midwest and north-west, where they began to wield substantial voting power. Though they did not necessarily admire Wilhelm II, they overwhelmingly favoured neutrality.

They feared – with good reason, moreover – that war with Germany would damage their community and took an actively neutralist position.

The third large demographic group consisted of the Irish, who had mostly settled on the East Coast. Following the destruction of harvests by the potato disease and subsequent famine, emigration from Ireland rapidly increased in the late 1840s. The attitude of these predominantly Catholic immigrants was profoundly shaped by the ongoing debate in Great Britain regarding the political status of Ireland, a subject that had grown considerably more bitter over the course of the twenty preceding years. In early 1914, no one in Great Britain seriously believed that the country could be dragged into a European war. By contrast, the question of Home Rule for Ireland – that is, of the country's autonomy – seriously divided British society. At the time, many feared that a civil war would break out in Ireland and that it might spread to the great industrial English cities. Given these circumstances, Irish-origin Americans generally held a dim view of Great Britain.

There was a fourth group of immigrants with some influence: Jews from central Europe and Russia. Beginning in the late nineteenth century, huge numbers of them immigrated to the United States, as much a reflection of the discrimination, mistreatment and even persecution to which they were subjected in their countries of origin as of the possibilities offered by the country's rapidly growing economy. These newcomers headed for large cities, taking jobs in factories and helping to expand urban small industry. The fact that pogromist tsarist Russia figured in the ranks of the Entente alongside France and Britain heavily influenced their assessment of events, at least until March 1917.[32] As the conflict dragged on, accounts began to spread in the United States of the frequent extortion committed by tsarist troops, particularly Cossack units, against Jewish populations near the battlefield. This also coloured their view.

A fifth large group of recent immigrants consisted of Italians. Most came from the peninsula's south and took up residence in north-eastern cities, often alongside heavily Irish areas (people with whom they shared their Catholic faith). Their arrival was still too recent to permit political influence at the national level. What's more, Italy was in principle allied with Germany and Austro-Hungary in 1914. When the war broke out, it chose to remain neutral but in 1915 entered the conflict on the Allied side.

Finally, of course, African Americans, Hispanics and Amerindians constituted a significant part of the population. At the time, however, these groups had virtually no political say in regards to the country's possible participation in the war in Europe, even if some (particularly among African Americans) hoped to win social and political promotion by enlisting in the military when the time came. As we shall see, such hopes would soon be disappointed.

In addition to the reluctance of various ethnic groups regarding American involvement in the war, one must take into account the country's very large and influential pacifist movement. The fact that it consisted of a set of fairly distinct currents only increased its impact at the national level.

First and foremost was a conservative religious current very active in the moral reform of the social norms to which most Protestant religious denominations subscribed.[33] Various synods of Presbyterian and Baptist churches came out strongly against any type of involvement in the war.

A heavily agrarian populist religious current, for its part, also had considerable influence in the southern and western United States. It was represented, among others, by William Jennings Bryan. A politician from Nebraska, Bryan was a liberal pacifist and Christian fundamentalist who steadfastly opposed all forms of American imperialism. A thrice-defeated Democratic presidential candidate, in 1912 Bryan endorsed Woodrow

Wilson as the party's candidate. The latter went on to win the nomination following a particularly contentious Democratic convention. In exchange, Wilson made Bryan his Secretary of State.[34] Among Republicans, this current was represented by a similarly colourful figure, Robert La Follette, an agrarian populist tribune and, for twenty years, senator from Wisconsin.[35]

At the same time, the rapid development of American industry resulted in a growing working class, many of whose members were recent immigrants. Sceptical towards the governments of central and Eastern Europe, which many of them had fled, they provided the base for a socialist and anarcho-syndicalist current. While this refractory current was in a state of perpetual reorganization, as a whole it staunchly opposed the 'imperialist war' in 1914. In 1916, Socialist Party of America candidate Eugene Debs was to receive more than a million votes.

As in Great Britain, there also existed a strong, fundamentally pacifist feminist movement. The only member of the House of Representatives who voted against the United States' entry into the war was Jeannette Rankin, a feminist politician from Minnesota (this at a time when women still did not have the right to vote in federal elections). In contrast to Great Britain, however, where the better part of the feminist movement rallied for national unity behind its leader, Emmeline Pankhurst, at least for a time, the American feminist movement for the most part continued to oppose the war for its entire duration.[36]

At the other end of the social and economic spectrum, a specific pacifist current traversed the political and economic elites.

For them – and, in particular, President Woodrow Wilson (1856–1924) – the decision to go to war on the part of European nations was just another sign of their profound political backwardness. With his election in 1912, Wilson, the son of a Presbyterian minister, was the first president of the United States to have come from the south since 1848. A professor of political science, he was also the first (and still only) president to hold a doctorate, and presided over the prestigious Princeton University before launching his political career in 1910 as governor of the state of New Jersey. In 1912, he was nominated by the Democratic convention in the forty-seventh round of voting. By temperament and education, he was a man of strong convictions and clear-cut opinions. Born in Virginia just before the Civil War, he witnessed the horrors of conflict as a child. For him, there was no question of the United States consenting to the immense backwards step that this war represented, at once an ethical failing and a human, economic and political disaster. Like Wilson himself, many of his supporters saw themselves as participants in the 'manifest destiny' that Tocqueville ascribed to American democracy... something that clearly did not involve rushing into the absurd, bloody and suicidal fray in which the nations of Europe were then engaged. On the contrary, the role of the United States was to ensure that the voice of reason be heard and possibly to work towards the conflict's peaceful resolution.

Finally, in a world (already) undergoing globalization and in which economic growth was driven by the expansion of international trade (a domain in which the United States played an ever-larger role), the war was bad for business... For many industrialists, the United States could of course agree to equip the belligerents in this deplorable conflict but it must observe total neutrality and in particular continue (for reasons of fairness, interest and prudence) to trade with all parties. In 1915, the most extreme of them, Henry Ford, went so far as to pay for a ship to be sent to Europe. Baptized the 'Peace Ship', Ford boarded it with more than 170 pacifist figures. Their objective was to sail to the ports of the various European countries, where they would disembark to engage leaders and public opinion. The idea was also to inspire the emergence of local pacifist movements capable of forcing their respective governments to put an end to the fighting. The expedition was a total failure. None of the warring countries allowed the boat to dock, and so, after a stopover in Amsterdam, a neutral port, it definitively ended its voyage in Sweden. From there, its passengers were repatriated on commercial ships.[37]

In a message to Congress delivered on 19 August 1914, Wilson asked his compatriots to remain impartial 'in thought as well as action'. He was moreover aware that one in seven Americans had been born in one of the countries now at war and that the electorate was profoundly divided over the subject. His message was well received by the press and public opinion in general. At the time, in any case, the United States was in absolutely no position to intervene militarily, at least not in the short term.

# CHAPTER 6

## THE AMERICAN ARMY BEFORE IT ENTERED THE WAR

At the end of the Civil War (1861–65), the United States drastically reduced the size of its standing armed forces in order to devote the bulk of its public resources to the country's reconstruction and development.

Following thirty years of massive immigration, in August 1914 the population of the United States exceeded 100 million inhabitants. Yet its armed forces consisted of barely 120,000 men, together with an additional 240,000 National Guard troops from the individual states.[38] Moreover, the country was virtually incapable of rapidly deploying this embryonic army. Of the 120,000 soldiers in the regular army, 21,000 were already stationed in the Philippines, 10,000 in Hawaii, 13,000 in Puerto Rico, 13,000 in China and a thousand in Alaska.[39] Within the continental United States, most troops were concentrated along the Mexican border, where they attempted – with no great success – to curb the activities of the revolutionary bandits Pancho Villa and Emiliano Zapata. A large portion of those remaining were assigned to coastal defence in anticipation of a hypothetical German, Japanese or even British naval attack.

No measures had been taken to conduct a census of military-age men, nor was there any system for conscripting them.[40] Held in low regard and poorly remunerated, a career in the military offered very few opportunities for social ascension. The army had no general staff in the modern sense of the term, much less an established strategic and tactical doctrine concerning the use of force. Since the Civil War, the American military experience had been limited to fighting the Sioux and Cheyenne tribes, Mexican irregulars, Filipino bandits and (in Cuba) a small contingent of the Spanish army.

But there was one exception: the US Navy. Thanks to the influence of Alfred Mahan, a professor of strategy at the US Naval Academy in Annapolis, the number and quality of its ships considerably increased in the late nineteenth century. Mahan's book, *The Influence of Sea Power upon History*, created a considerable stir in military and political circles, not just in the United States but also in Great Britain, Germany and Japan.[41] Briefly, Mahan took note of the fact that naval warfare had undergone profound technological transformation, with the simultaneous development of steam power, large-calibre, long-range cannon and hermetic metallic armour. Henceforth, a great country's fleet could massively and decisively intervene on the other side of the planet provided it had access to coal-supply bases around the world. The possession of a fleet of modern battleships and the mastery of the oceans it provided thus became an essential element of a country's power, economic development and security. Mahan's theories were well received by some American politicians, first and foremost Theodore Roosevelt. Under his presidency (1900–4), a programme was launched to make the United States the world's third-largest naval power behind Great Britain and Germany. At the same time, the United States took steps to increase the number of its naval bases in the Caribbean, the Pacific (Hawaii) and Asia (the Philippines) so as to ensure its fleet could resupply throughout the world.

That said, after Roosevelt left the White House in 1904, military spending fell, with predictable consequences for new construction and the upkeep and operation of existing ships.

In 1914, the American fleet was short of crew and possessed a disproportionate number of massive battleships, which were costly to construct and maintain.[42] These mastodons had been built in anticipation of a need to fight enemy fleets on the high seas. By contrast, the US Navy was under-equipped in destroyers and rapid-escort ships, which play such an important role in ensuring the security of maritime lines of communication.

In 1914, the United States thus had neither armed land forces capable of intervening in Europe nor the naval resources needed to transport them there. In this respect, it was no different from the nations of the British Empire, which generally lacked a national army in the true sense of the term but which nevertheless immediately threw themselves into the war alongside Great Britain (with, it is true, the support of the British fleet).

More astonishing yet, over the course of the next three years, as the conflict in Europe dragged on and quickly assumed an unprecedented form and intensity, very little was done to prepare the American army for the possibility that it might enter the war. Preparedness became the object of at once intense and acrimonious national debate, its terms evolving as the conflict dragged on.[43]

Yet, for all that, the American army of the time was not lacking in talent: it was in these years that, among others, George C. Marshall, Douglas MacArthur and George S. Patton began their careers as officers. It would only be in the course of the following conflict, however, that they would truly have a chance to prove their mettle.

# CHAPTER 7

## THE UNITED STATES SLIDES INTO WAR

Between 1914 and 1917, two fields strongly influenced the stance taken by the United States towards the conflict. First of all, the evolution of international trade. The late nineteenth and early twentieth centuries witnessed the first great wave of modern globalization, a phenomenon marked by rapidly expanding commerce. For the American, French, British and German economies, this was precisely accompanied by growing dependence on (mainly seaborne) international trade, which was essential for the supply of local industry and to ensure that national products could access their natural markets. Contrary to the socialist theories of the time, which above all imagined the forthcoming war as an opportunity for industrialists to make money while breaking the workers' movement, this was one reason why French, British and German business circles responded with such little enthusiasm to the outbreak of hostilities in 1914.

This was also a concern among military planners. On the eve of the war, the German general staff under Helmuth

Johannes Ludwig von Moltke, often referred to as 'Moltke the Younger', thus significantly modified the Schlieffen Plan, which had originally been developed in the late 1890s. The plan provided for invading France through Belgium. Initially, it anticipated simultaneously invading Belgium and the Netherlands so as to clear the largest possible corridor for advancing German troops, allowing a maximum number to head westwards across the Rhine in as little time as possible. But though his plan sought rapidly to conclude hostilities (which were projected to last no more than three months), Moltke nevertheless wished to respect Dutch neutrality. At all costs, he wanted to retain an Atlantic port for German industrial supplies and exports. By safeguarding Dutch neutrality, he thus hoped to preserve the operational capacity of the port of Rotterdam to supply Germany.

As we saw in the previous chapter, at the outbreak of hostilities American public opinion did not side with any of the belligerents. Nevertheless, despite lingering reservations in some quarters regarding Great Britain, the public's sympathy for the democracies of France and Britain and the tiny invaded nation of Belgium was markedly greater than anything aroused by the Central Powers. News of the atrocities committed by German troops against civilian populations rapidly spread, particularly following the arrival of the first American war correspondents on the scene in late August 1914, which gave the stories more credibility.[44] Yet the vast majority of Americans thought that it was the ethical duty of the United States, as well as in its economic and political interests, to stay neutral, even if German violence against civilians during the invasion of Belgium exacerbated the latent anti-German sentiment of many Americans. The reality of German atrocities in Belgium soon became a matter of controversy, one that lingers to this day to some degree. On both sides, propaganda organizations, with support from the press, selectively interpreted facts in a biased and hyperbolic manner. Yet American public opinion squarely laid the blame for the conflict's brutalization at the Germans' feet, for the most part rightly so.[45]

At the same time, American national and material interests were affected by Germany's decision to embark on an unprecedented form of naval warfare – submarine warfare. From the beginning of the conflict, the two camps sought to blockade their rivals' maritime supply routes. When, to general surprise, the war carried on beyond the winter, these efforts only intensified. Given the evolution of modern weaponry, all expected a very violent conflict in the summer of 1914. But its very intensity would supposedly limit its duration by rapidly exhausting available human and material resources. However, the rapid conversion of European economies to a war footing allowed the stockpiles of materiel and munitions consumed by the war effort to be replenished at a rate never imagined by military planners. The conflict thus continued. By the same token, huge quantities of raw materials had to be imported to feed wartime production. What's more, since male agricultural workers had been called up and would remain in service for many years, feeding soldiers and civilians gradually came to require that food be imported. Horses and draught animals had also been massively mobilized to supply the needs of what in 1914 was an almost entirely horse-drawn army, and one that in 1918 would largely remain so. These animals suffered very high casualties.[46] Despite the contributions of women, children and the elderly, the productivity of European agriculture thus declined.

In this respect, the two parties to the conflict were in a very asymmetric situation. While the French and especially the British fleets were able to establish an effective blockade of North Sea ports by laying mines and inspecting ships in the Channel, the German surface navy could not do so for the Allies' Atlantic ports. Though it had rapidly grown in the twenty years preceding the war, the German fleet in fact only left its ports in strength on a single – destructive but inconclusive – occasion: the Battle of Jutland in 1915. The British surface fleet was thus able to inspect German or neutral ships coming or going from German ports. In an effort to interrupt maritime traffic on the North Atlantic, Germany thus decided to use its submarine fleet (U-boats). While it initially possessed few submarines, construction soon accelerated. In order to inspect a commercial vessel, however, a U-boat had to come to the surface and make its intentions known. If, as would soon be the case, the commercial ship was armed, the submarine, with little surface mobility, became easy prey in its turn. To avoid this risk, the German general staff thus decided to break with the conventions of international maritime law and torpedo without warning hostile or neutral ships navigating in a zone of exclusion defined beforehand.[47]

In applying this doctrine, on 7 May 1915 a U-boat torpedoed and sank the British ocean liner *Lusitania* within sight of the British coast, resulting in the death by drowning of 1,198 people, including 128 American citizens. This was not the only time American citizens died after their ship was torpedoed, but the *Lusitania* was by far the deadliest such incident. In response, Wilson demanded reparations and apologies from Germany as well as a cessation of unconditional submarine warfare. It must nevertheless be noted that, in his formal protest to Germany, Wilson did not directly threaten intervention in the conflict but only the possibility that diplomatic relations would be severed. Yet even this was too much for his Secretary of State, William Jennings Bryan. Fiercely neutralist, Bryan saw Wilson's position as too partial and feared that it might drag the United States into the conflict. He believed that the United States should place greater pressure on Great Britain to relax its blockade policy and allow the United States to trade freely with Germany. He thus resigned dramatically in June 1915. Sensitive to American pressure, Germany gradually scaled back its submarine war against neutral and belligerent ships. In May 1916, it formally suspended the programme.

In fact, the Royal Navy was capable of blockading the enemy coast. The *Kriegsmarine*, for its part, could not do so without resorting to all-out submarine warfare, something for which it reckoned it lacked the military and diplomatic resources.

As a neutral power, the United States was theoretically ready to trade with all of the warring parties. Since the British blockade had made it impossible for American ships to penetrate the North Sea, however, US trade with Germany rapidly collapsed. In 1916, it was at just 1 per cent of its 1914 level. Over the same period, trade with Great Britain and France tripled.[48]

As the commercial ties linking the United States, France and Britain grew stronger, so, too, did their financial relationships. From January 1915, the bank J. P. Morgan, at the time directed by J. P. Morgan, Jr, the founder's very Anglophile son, became the exclusive agent of the British government in the United States for financing and concluding supply contracts with the United Kingdom. In the two years that followed, these represented a total of more than 3 billion dollars. Similarly, the house of Morgan and its branch in Paris facilitated French Treasury and bank access to American capital markets. In the space of two years, the United States ceased being generally in debt to Europe and increasingly became the latter's creditor – the first time this had happened since the nation's founding. It naturally became more sensitive to the fate of its new debtors, France and Great Britain. Conversely, it acquired a position of significant influence over the policy choices made by the leaders of these two countries.

In keeping with his deep ethical and intellectual convictions, over the course of his first term in office Woodrow Wilson launched several initiatives to bring the belligerents to the negotiation table. This was not without precedent, moreover, as the United States had in the recent past acted as mediator in another major conflict. In 1904, the then president, Theodore Roosevelt, arranged to mediate between the Russians and the Japanese, who were at the time involved in a very bloody war, the first to witness the use (to devastating effect) of modern weaponry. In 1905, his efforts resulted in the signing at Portsmouth, New Hampshire, of a peace treaty between the two empires. The following year, Roosevelt received the Nobel Peace Prize for this success. Wilson aimed to emulate the success of his old political opponent.

In his diplomatic efforts, he could not rely upon his Secretary of State, William Jennings Bryan, whose views were the complete contrary of his own. It was thus one of his personal friends, Colonel Edward M. House, whom he charged with the responsibility for an official mission to explore the conditions placed by the belligerents on suspending hostilities.[49] House's first trip to Europe took place in 1915. His mission was interrupted almost immediately by the crisis provoked by the torpedoing of the *Lusitania*, and he returned to Washington DC to present the situation. In the view of Bryan, titular Secretary of State, House excessively favoured the British, a view that contributed to Bryan's decision to resign. Nothing more concrete was achieved by a second trip to Europe in early 1916. This was at the time of the Battle of Verdun and preparations were underway for that of the Somme. Neither of the two coalitions wished to indicate their possible willingness to begin discussions, however preliminary or indirect, until they had made material gains on the ground.

As the conflict dragged on, Wilson began to worry that it might lead to the total collapse of the warring powers on both sides and for many years. Such an outcome would be at once morally unacceptable and economically and politically dangerous for the United States.

In late 1916, the war raged on in Europe and debate continued in the United States regarding its possible consequences for the country. Without necessarily supporting armed intervention, some argued for upgrading federal military forces in keeping with the lessons of the ongoing conflict. By contrast, others underscored the fact that US territory was in no way threatened. For them, any expansion or modernization of the American armed forces was merely the first step on a path that mechanically led to war. Some took pleasure in the fact that the United States was for the time being the conflict's principal beneficiary. With their European economic and political rivals in the process of self-destructing, the American economy was running at full throttle and the considerable gold reserves of Britain and France were headed for the United States. As the conflict evolved, however, the possibility of German victory was increasingly feared in the United States. Alongside the fundamentally less democratic nature of the Central Powers compared to their Western rivals, Americans began to worry about the danger that triumphant German militarism would pose for them.

For their part, those who favoured American involvement in the conflict did not remain inactive. Supported by Theodore Roosevelt, they launched the 'Preparedness Movement': since civilian and military authorities obstinately refused to prepare the country, particularly its young people, for the forthcoming conflict, private individuals would have to take responsibility for this effort. They financed the creation of private military training centres, the first of which established in Plattsburgh, Pennsylvania. Beginning in 1915, many students from the East Coast, including several hundred from Harvard and Yale, travelled there to attend military preparation courses.

The more the conflict in Europe became bogged down, the more the debate in the United States regarding the country's level of military expenditure intensified. The most determined partisans of neutrality saw to it that this expenditure in no way increased, persuaded as they were that the unpreparedness of the US Army constituted a fundamental obstacle to entering the war. Conversely, they were convinced that any effort to expand the armed forces would make American intervention inevitable by making it possible.

Astonishingly, the question of the United States' possible involvement in the conflict was not really central to the presidential election of November 1916. It is true that, running on the Democrat ticket for re-election, Wilson partly campaigned on the slogan 'He kept us out of the war!' But facing him was a Republican Party profoundly divided between an interventionist wing led by Theodore Roosevelt and a deeply isolationist faction personified by Robert La Follette, the populist senator from Wisconsin. In the event, Wilson decisively defeated his Republican opponent, Charles Evans Hughes, a former Supreme Court Justice.

In December 1916, just one month after being re-elected, Wilson opened a new round of secret consultations with the warring parties regarding the conditions for a possible armistice. In late January, he felt sufficiently satisfied with the feedback reaching him to announce publicly a major peace initiative before the US Senate. In a speech on 22 January 1917 entitled 'Peace without Victory', Wilson stated that he had received constructive responses from all belligerents to his queries regarding the acceptable terms for an immediate cessation to hostilities under current circumstances. He thus anticipated that decisive negotiations would rapidly get under way under the aegis of the United States. Wilson's aim was to find a way to end the war that would not require one camp to have militarily, materially or morally crushed the other first. Moreover, he counted on bringing the French and British to the negotiating table thanks to the influence conferred upon him by the fact that the United States was their principal creditor.

Yet he was unaware of the fact that, even as he made these public statements, Germany's leaders had already decided to resume unrestricted submarine warfare. For the moment silent on the subject, their constantly expanded and modernized U-boat fleet was taking up position in the Atlantic. Their decision would be made public on 31 January 1917.

# CHAPTER 8

## THE GERMAN GENERAL STAFF'S STRATEGIC GAMBLE

Over the course of the First World War, the German general staff took a series of risky strategic gambles. The first of these was to implement the Schlieffen Plan – the invasion of France by way of Belgium in August 1914. This meant concentrating almost all of their forces on the Western Front, leaving only a thin curtain of troops to defend the east on the assumption that much time would be needed for Russia to fully mobilize its immense army. The plan's successful execution depended on many factors: that the French troops massed along the frontier with Alsace-Lorraine would be rapidly encircled from the west; that an intimidated Belgian government would grant safe passage to German troops; that the invasion of Belgium would not trigger Great Britain's entry into the war, even though it was a signatory (together with France and Germany) to the Treaty of London guaranteeing Belgian neutrality; and finally that German troops, as in 1870, would require no more than six weeks to beat the French army decisively and rapidly once contact had been made. One after the other, the Germans lost each of these gambles.

Yet this did not prevent the German general staff from contemplating a major new strategic gamble in early 1917. Since the onset of hostilities, German military and political leaders were split over the question of whether to use their U-boat fleet to block all forms of North Atlantic maritime traffic, neutral or otherwise, headed for France or (especially) Great Britain. The leaders of the German admiralty assured the Kaiser that their submarine fleet was capable of massively reducing trade in the direction of the Allied nations. They were confident that within three to six months an effective blockade could force the Allies to sue for an end to hostilities.[50] The German chancellor, Theobald von Bethmann Hollweg, was not in the least convinced. Indeed, he particularly worried that resuming submarine warfare would drag the United States into the conflict, possibly tipping the demographic and industrial scales in the Allies' favour. He also feared the impact that such a decision might have on Germany's relations with neutral European states such as the Netherlands, Denmark, Sweden and Spain. At this stage of the war, these countries played a minor but significant role in Germany's ability to retain some connection with international trade. The position of German high command leaders – Erich von Falkenhayn first and then Hindenburg and Ludendorff from summer 1916 – fluctuated with the evolving fortunes of war. In the middle of this group of leaders, Kaiser Wilhelm II, the ultimate decision-maker, long hesitated between what became ever more divergent positions.

At the end of 1916, a year that witnessed the failure of the Verdun offensive (launched by the Germans) and that of the Somme (launched by the Allies), Hindenburg and Ludendorff, now in charge of the high command, were convinced that the nature of the conflict had changed. The search for the decisive battle and a breakthrough of enemy lines had been replaced by a war of attrition in both human and materiel terms. In the view of these strategists, this new form of warfare put Germany in a fundamentally disadvantageous position – as long, that is, as the nation continued to be subjected to the Allies' trade and shipping blockade without interrupting or even restricting the latter's supply of agricultural and industrial raw material and equipment of all kinds.[51]

In fact, not only was the Allied war machine well supplied, but agricultural imports also spared the populations of France and Britain most of the deprivations and rationing to which German civilians were increasingly subjected. And though German soldiers continued to be properly supplied at the front, their (infrequent) periods of leave made them aware of the growing restrictions imposed upon their families, which in turn could affect their morale. In short, the German general staff had come to doubt their ability to achieve a decisive victory over the Allies and began to consider ways in which the mutual exhaustion of combatants on both sides could be used to put an end to the conflict, but on a basis that favoured Germany. To that end, recourse to submarine warfare seemed very tempting.

Ludendorff concluded from this that it was now crucial to disrupt maritime trade on the Atlantic seriously by resuming unrestricted submarine warfare. He was thus prepared for the risk that this would once and for all push the United States into the war.

On 9 January 1917, the German military leadership met with the chancellor in Royal Council, with the Kaiser presiding. Their message was simple: 'Either we immediately and massively resume submarine warfare or we lose the war.' In some ways anticipating the 'stab-in-the-back' metaphor, they darkly added that, in case of a contrary decision, Germany's military leadership would in no way share responsibility for the forthcoming defeat...[52]

Shaken, the Kaiser gave in and signed the order to resume

total submarine warfare beginning on 1 February 1917, and this without negotiating with or notifying foreign powers in advance. As Chancellor Bethmann Hollweg bitterly noted: 'It is the end of Germany!'

This decision entailed five new gambles, all interrelated and all connected with the reaction of the United States:

- a gamble that the United States, where public opinion continued to be divided (though the Central Powers now had a very bad image), would once again content itself with diplomatic protests, as after the sinking of the *Lusitania*;
- a gamble that, even if it formally entered the war this time, the United States would not go so far as to send massive numbers of troops to Europe but rather limit itself to sending a symbolic expeditionary corps;
- a gamble that, even if the United States decided to intervene massively on the European front, its unpreparedness meant that it would take at least eighteen months or even two years before its troops were operational;
- a gamble that any effort to equip a newly formed American army would necessarily come at the expense of shipments to its allies;
- a gamble, finally – which in case of success would justify all others – that German submarines would actually succeed in interrupting or at least seriously disrupting the maritime traffic of men and merchandise on the North Atlantic. Germany would thus have succeeded in weakening the Allied war machine and slowing – or even preventing – the intervention of US troops in Europe.

As before, these successive gambles were lost one after another. Between April and June 1917, German submarines destroyed Allied and neutral ships amounting to 2.2 million tons (including 885,000 in May alone), or roughly eighty allied or neutral ships. But the success of this offensive quickly waned. The main factor of this decline was the Allies' successful adoption of a convoy-based system for ships crossing the North Atlantic. Protected by fast destroyer escorts (American, British and Canadian), it became much more difficult for U-boats to strike commercial vessels. At the same time, the U-boats themselves became more vulnerable to the torpedoes and depth charges launched by the swarming destroyers. Sunken tonnage rapidly dropped to 300,000 tons a month, while the number of German submarines that were sunk significantly increased. Finally, production of new troop- and materiel-transport ships skyrocketed in American shipyards. Beginning in early 1918, the construction of new ships more than compensated for losses at sea.[53]

Above all, the system of convoys that escorted the swarm of transport ships and ocean liners (including the *France* and *Queen Mary* of the day) allowed around 2.1 million soldiers (and their equipment) to be transported between May 1917 and November 1918, and this with almost no losses as a result of German submarine activity. This was a source of huge disappointment in Germany, particularly as this tactical failure was accompanied by strategic disaster: US entry into the war.

The feeling that he had been misled by his German contacts over the course of the conversations that took place in the autumn of 1916 regarding a possible cessation of hostilities figured heavily in Wilson's decision to ask Congress to declare war on Germany. And, if that did not suffice, the discovery of a German initiative encouraging Mexico to declare war on the United States decisively swayed American political leaders and public opinion alike.

For, realizing that the upcoming resumption of submarine warfare might drag the United States into the war, on 17 January 1917 the German minister of foreign affairs, Arthur

Zimmermann, sent a coded telegram to his ambassador in Mexico. It asked him to propose that the Mexican government join the German coalition and attack the United States. In addition to financial and material support, the Germans offered to recuperate and return the territory Mexico had lost in the nineteenth century: Texas, New Mexico and Arizona.

To make matters worse, the document suggested that this backhanded alliance against the United States might eventually be expanded to include Japan. And this at a time when Japan, which had entrusted the modernization of its army to German instructors, was increasingly a source of concern to the Americans due to its trans-Pacific activism.

The message was intercepted by the British, who had tapped the underwater telegraphic wire between Europe and the United States. They succeeded in deciphering the message and in late February passed it along to the US authorities, who in turn made it public in early March. Its effect on public opinion was predictable.[54]

Woodrow Wilson was now convinced that the 'peace without victory' he hoped and prayed for was fundamentally unacceptable to the Reich. It was thus only possible if the United States entered the war, decisively contributing to the Allies' victory and thereby putting itself in a position to impose peace terms and lay the groundwork for the new, liberal and democratic European order that was be constructed. It was Wilson's ambition to be the architect of this new world order.

On 2 April 1917, President Wilson jointly addressed both chambers of Congress. Faced with German aggression, he asked that Congress recognize the existence of a 'state of war' between Germany and the United States.

On 6 April – the official date of the United States' entry into the war – Congress voted in favour of the motion by a very large majority, albeit not unanimously (eighty-two votes for and six against in the Senate, with eight senators abstaining, and 373 versus fifty in the House of Representatives).[55] Some representatives (who nevertheless supported the motion) expressed reservations in the course of the debate. As Claude Kitchin, leader of the House Democratic majority, remarked: 'I will always believe that we could have and should have stayed out of this conflict.' In addition to La Follette (senator from Wisconsin), two other 'progressive Republicans' representing western states (North Dakota and Nebraska) took the floor to speak against the war motion. They were joined by two Democratic senators from the Deep South, representing Mississippi and Missouri, respectively.

In his speech to Congress, Wilson thus defined American war aims via an ambiguous formula, the success of which continues to this day: 'to make the world safer for democracy'. It must nevertheless be emphasized that the United States abstained from formally joining the Allied coalition against the Central Powers. It was solely a matter of acknowledging a 'state of war' with Germany and Germany alone. A war that the United States counted on waging by and for itself, even if it hoped to coordinate its actions with the Franco-British forces. As Wilson put it, the United States was not 'allied' with Great Britain and France in their fight against Germany but rather merely 'associated'. It would nevertheless ultimately declare war on Austro-Hungary nine months later, on 7 December 1917. The aim in doing so was to come to the aid of Italy, which had joined the Allied side in 1915 and had just experienced a major military setback in the Battle of Caporetto.[56] The United States never declared war on Germany's other two allies, Turkey and Bulgaria.

The Americans thus entered the war in April 1917 on their own terms, those chosen by Woodrow Wilson.

# CHAPTER 9

## PREPARING THE AMERICAN INTERVENTION

In April 1917, it was far from obvious that America's decision to intervene in the conflict would involve sending a massive expeditionary corps to Europe. Indeed, even many of those who favoured entering the war above all saw this as involving increased financial and material support, perhaps coupled with the dispatch of a symbolic group of volunteers.[57]

But Wilson's ultimate objective was to ensure that, once there had been a cessation of hostilities, the US government – and thus Wilson himself – would have a decisive say in defining the new world order destined to be established among the ruins of the old. To this end, it was not enough to serve as the democracies' arsenal or financier: Wilson was convinced that the United States had to play a decisive role on the battlefield as well. It was thus necessary to raise rapidly a mass army that could be sent to fight in Europe, and this on a very slim foundation.

Creating an army and sending millions of American soldiers with no experience into battle thousands of kilometres from home required taking a whole series of steps in succession – a task that depended on human, material and administrative resources in no way possessed by the United States when it first entered the war. Among other things, it was necessary:

- to conduct a census of the fighting-age male population;
- to recruit from among them the men one wished to enlist;
- to clothe, accommodate, feed and equip the new recruits;
- to supply them with basic military training;
- to transport them by ship to the other side of the Atlantic, together with their equipment;
- to provide them, behind the front lines in France and in Britain, with a minimum of training regarding the specific aspects of the fighting they were likely to see;[58]
- to organize them into coherent units capable of effective manoeuvre before sending them into battle;
- to develop a coherent doctrine of tactical deployment and force engagement as well as an experienced general staff.

Apart from the initial census, which took place without much incident, the implementation of each of these steps encountered major stumbling blocks.

The first step of the process therefore consisted in overseeing conscription in order to create a mass army not wholly dependent on volunteers. The use of conscription is not part of the American political tradition, for it is seen as a major violation of individual freedom on the part of the federal government. Indeed, the country's leading human-rights association, the American Civil Liberties Union (ACLU), had precisely been created to oppose its implementation. The Union and Confederacy had only made minor use of conscription during the Civil War. In early twentieth-century France, by contrast, the so-called 'blood tax' was a major republican principle at the foundation of a form of virtually universal conscription. Conscription also existed in Imperial Germany, but it was applied somewhat less rigorously. Germany's demographic momentum in the nineteenth century, coupled with an inverse trend in France, meant that, in 1914, the Second Reich's population was 50 per cent larger than that of France (60 million people versus fewer than 40 million). Exemptions were thus much more commonplace in Germany, covering students and, above all, particular social groups such as social-democratic workers, who it was believed were better off without too much weapons training...

In the United States, the dominant political culture was profoundly individualistic and hostile to all constraints that might be imposed by the central government.[59] Individual volunteering was celebrated instead. But, in the spring of 1917, Wilson was far from confident that a sufficient number of volunteers would present themselves. In contrast to the British volunteers of 1914, for example, Americans contemplating volunteering in 1917 made their decisions with advance knowledge of the horribly bloody nature of the conflict.

Conscription was thus formally established by the Selective Service Act signed by Wilson on 19 May 1917. Henceforth, every male American between the ages of twenty-one and thirty was obliged to register with his local recruitment office.[60] More than 4,500 offices were hastily set up. The day they opened, 5 June 1917, nearly 10 million young Americans presented themselves.[61] Few incidents were reported around the country, though several clashes were nevertheless noted with protesters in a handful of southern states, including Georgia, Tennessee and Alabama. Other problems were reported, often in the Midwest, where the followers of certain Protestant fundamentalist churches refused to bear arms as a matter of principle.

Over the course of the conflict, 24 million young Americans (out of a total male population of 54 million in

1917) nevertheless presented themselves for recruitment. Of this total, just 2,810,896 were actually conscripted. There are several explanations for this discrepancy. First of all, the exceptional size of the American fighting-age population and the large number of volunteers in absolute terms.[62] Next, the large number of exemption mechanisms. Everyone could claim an exemption on the grounds of family responsibility and many did. The government took care to avoid disrupting the operation of the arms industry and, more generally, any area that contributed to the national defence. The development of American industry and the rapid growth of an urban industrial proletariat produced the same consequences as in Europe for the health of the populations in question: many were exempted due to their poor physical condition. This is why those first conscripted largely consisted of young people from rural parts of the country. Surprisingly, a large number of men from the black community also volunteered. From the start of the conflict, however, several of black America's most radical leaders opposed entering a war between European imperialists that on the face of it in no way concerned them. Other historic civil rights activists such as W.E.B. Du Bois, by contrast, saw it as an exceptional opportunity to advance more rapidly the cause of racial equality within the American population. For what remained a mainly rural population of young blacks, what's more, military life seemed to offer a prospect for promotion and integration into the country's urban and industrial society.

Yet this hope was to be constantly and cruelly disappointed throughout the conflict. Black soldiers were assigned mainly material tasks (unloading boats, constructing new roads and railroads, and so on). The instructing officers, most of whom were southern whites, treated black recruits so rudely that incidents broke out at the gates of training camps. The most violent of these, which took place between black soldiers and white policemen in Houston on 23 August 1917, led the troops to revolt: infuriated by their ill treatment, black soldiers killed seventeen white civilians. There of course followed ferocious repression: 156 black soldiers were court-martialled and nineteen executed.[63]

The United States' entry into the war nevertheless had a very significant impact on the black population: it accelerated its geographical migration from the southern states, where it was mainly employed in agricultural labour, towards the industrial states of the north-east and the Great Lakes region. Factories had to operate at full capacity to feed the war effort, even though a portion of their labour force had volunteered or been mobilized. Above all, immigration, which had dried up since the beginning of the conflict, was no longer there to fill the empty places. Massive numbers of black labourers thus moved north, and this internal migration profoundly modified the geographical distribution of the African American population.

Paradoxically, the US Army had a completely different attitude towards American Indians, their historic adversaries. In contrast to black soldiers, many Indian-origin soldiers were integrated into fighting units and assigned reconnaissance tasks.[64]

Above all, American military planners knew that they were absolutely incapable of absorbing more recruits for the time being. Uniforms, weapons and equipment of all kinds were at first lacking. So, too, were sufficient numbers of officers and NCOs capable of instructing the recruits, even if it were merely a matter of how to march in step or respond to orders. This was the most difficult bottleneck for the American army to overcome. In April 1917, the 1,500 line officers and 100 or so general staff officers had only been trained to fight Indian tribes (the oldest among them) or Mexican irregulars (the youngest).

In eighteen months, the United States nevertheless succeeded in increasing the size of its armed forces thirty times over, going from 120,000 men in arms to more than 4 million.

Deciding how to go about organizing the new American army was not straightforward. To command the American Expeditionary Force (AEF), President Wilson chose Major General John Pershing (1860–1948). Yet Pershing was not the most senior or highest-ranking field officer. Having graduated from West Point in 1886, by 1917 he already had a long military career behind him. He served on all of the fronts where the US Army had been engaged over the course of this period: first the American Indian Wars, then the Spanish–American War (1898) and the subsequent expedition to the Philippines (1899–1901). He also stood out by virtue of having commanded a regiment of black recruits (the 10th Calvary Regiment, commonly known as the 'Buffalo Soldiers'). There, he won the nickname 'Black Jack' – not necessarily a compliment in the US Army of that time.

Pershing's military career continued to advance, particularly after he married the daughter of a Republican senator from Wyoming, Francis Warren, who, moreover, headed the Senate committee tasked with overseeing the military budget. He was appointed as the military attaché to Tokyo in 1905, which allowed him to observe the Russo-Japanese War from the Japanese side. Noticed by President Theodore Roosevelt, he was then expeditiously promoted to the rank of brigadier general. In 1914, the onset of the war found him in charge of US troops stationed in Texas to protect the border with Mexico.[65] In response to Pancho Villa's incursions, in 1916 he led a punitive expedition that drove deep into Mexican territory. After many difficulties, however, he failed to capture Villa.

In April 1917, following a brief meeting with Wilson, Pershing was put at the head of the future expeditionary corps in Europe.

Apart from his relationship with the president, he enjoyed near total autonomy relative to other American political leaders of the time. He could thus oversee the country's military involvement in the conflict more or less as he liked. Following the war, the secretary of war, Newton Baker, liked to recall how he only ever gave Pershing two orders: to go to Europe and then to come back.[66]

Yet before leaving for Saint-Nazaire in June 1917, Pershing received perfectly clear instructions directly from Woodrow Wilson:

> In military operations against the Imperial German government you are directed to cooperate with the forces of the other countries employed against that enemy: but in so doing the underlying idea must be kept in view that the forces of the United States are a separate and distinct component of the combined forces, the identity of which must be preserved.[67]

What is certain is that, provided he conformed to the guiding principle laid out above, Pershing hardly needed to fear political interference in leading the AEF on European territory. The instructions he received thus perfectly suited both his philosophy and his immediate intentions.

As US troops began to arrive in Europe, the first dilemma confronting him concerned their possible integration into pre-existing French and British units. This, in any case, is what Allied political leaders proposed. At this stage of the war, they knew that their own units were physically and morally exhausted, particularly following the Chemin des Dames, Ypres and Passchendaele offensives. Moreover, the demographic reservoir provided the Allies by their various empires was beginning to run dry, resulting in a growing use of conscription in the British dominions. Getting American soldiers to the front line was thus a matter of urgency.[68]

However, the soldiers who had begun to land in France in the autumn of 1917 required a minimum of training in the particularities of trench warfare before being dispatched to the front line. As we have seen, because of its very small size, the US Army possessed few experienced junior officers to train the millions of inexperienced conscripts and volunteers who had joined the ranks. For the Allied military leaders, the most rapid and efficient solution seemed to be to combine the newcomers with small groups (at company level, for example) of French and British troops at rest. In this way, they might receive their basic military training from experienced instructors. Their numbers might subsequently rise in these units, where, as with new French or British troops, they would be immediately taken in hand by 'old hands' who would initiate them in the gestures, equipment, 'reflexes' and tactics they needed to confront the enemy while preserving a chance of survival. Finally – an additional advantage – directly integrating American troops into existing French and British units would reduce the quantity of materiel and specific equipment that had to be transferred to Europe. The (all too scarce) ships available might then carry more men on each trip, thereby reducing the time necessary to transport the bulk of the US Army to Europe.

This was precisely what the French and British diplomatic–military missions, respectively led by former prime minister René Viviani and Field Marshal Joseph Joffre (for the French) and Lord Balfour and General Tom Bridges (for the British), had just proposed in Washington.[69]

For Pershing, all of this was out of the question.

First, the idea was entirely contrary to the explicit instructions he had received from his political principals, starting with President Wilson. In observing Wilson's instruction to preserve the autonomy of the AEF, Pershing enjoyed total protection at the political level. By virtue of the decisive victories to come, the US Army would put the United States in its rightful place

– the leading one – at the table of future negotiations. Above all, it was unacceptable to transform the expeditionary corps into a reservoir of back-up troops intended to fill the huge gaps that more than three years of bloody fighting had created in the Allied armies. In any case, it would have been impossible to explain to the American public that its boys would serve as cannon fodder for foreign (albeit Allied) armies.

Personally, Pershing had of course no interest in a strategy that would have effectively deprived him of his role as commander-in-chief of the American armies and confined him to the role of a sort of high-ranking quartermaster general. Pershing had, moreover, arrived in France with his own philosophy of combat, one that he considered better suited to what he took to be the nature of the American soldier and more likely to bring final victory than the tactics implemented by the Allies. He called this concept 'open warfare'. For, in Pershing's view, the American soldier was absolutely not made for huddling in trenches, leaving the battle's outcome to be decided by heavy artillery duels: naturally given to the open country, he was intrinsically aggressive and above all used his great mastery of his individual weapon to win in battle. Oddly, Pershing's philosophy largely overlapped with that of the French military commanders of 1914 – that of the 'all-out attack' (but assigning the rifle the role that the instructors of France's war college had attributed to the bayonet), which, it was claimed, historically suited the French 'race' and its tradition of *furia francese*.

Pershing was convinced that the AEF was called upon to win victory over Germany not just by supplying the Allies with 2, 3 or even 4 million additional soldiers, but by extricating the conflict from the war of trenches and materiel in which it had become bogged down.

On the basis of this conviction, Pershing took two fundamental decisions regarding the organization of his troops in France.

The first was to consolidate his forces into large infantry divisions, each consisting of 28,000 men. This was twice the size of a French infantry division. The idea was that, once engaged in an offensive, an American infantry division had to possess a sufficiently large number of men to pursue its effort as long as possible without being relieved. Moreover, the ratio of officers to rank-and-file soldiers was lower than among the French and British, a logical step given the small number of officers available to Pershing. In order to retain some mobility, finally, American divisions were equipped with the same number of artillery pieces as their French counterparts. Proportionally to the number of soldiers, the Americans thus possessed only half as many artillery pieces as the French.

Pershing also gave thought to the location in which his armies would be positioned on the front. After an inspection tour in the late summer of 1917, he opted for a portion of the Lorraine front east of Verdun and across from Metz. This zone was located along the Franco-German border of 1871 and relatively close to the Rhine. For Pershing's final objective was to achieve what French and British military leaders had been unable to do since the start of the war: resume the war of movement, break through German lines and, finally, take the war into German territory across the Rhine. Given the time needed to transport and train his troops, Pershing hoped to be in a position to launch a decisive offensive in spring 1919. He was convinced that, if the conflict had become bogged down since 1914, this was not due to the capacity of modern weaponry to prevent infantry from advancing over open ground. Rather, he saw the bloody stalemate into which the fighting had descended as above all the result – even if he did not put it in so many words – of the incompetence and moral and intellectual exhaustion of Allied military leaders.

It was a feeling broadly shared by the American political elites of the time, who regarded their European counterparts – civilian and military alike – with a mix of condescension and dismay for having allowed their respective countries to take part in a suicidal war that under their leadership had devolved into endless butchery.

Things were thus going to change. The time had come...

Before that, however, troops and materiel had to be transported to France and its training camps. One consequence of the decision taken by American military and political leaders to operate with an expeditionary force distinct from and independent of the French and British armies was the pushing back – and that for many months – of the moment when large numbers of American soldiers took part in the fighting. For if American troops had been immediately combined with already existing Allied units, the United States could have fairly rapidly dispatched front-line infantry troops – something urgently requested by the Allies from the spring of 1917. Conversely, the US Army's decision to operate autonomously required that the entire military infrastructure of a modern army be recruited and transferred to Europe: equipment trains, armourers, quartermasters, cooks, hospitals, accountants, and so on. It took time to establish these systems and boats to transport men and materiel.

And, indeed, local inhabitants were much impressed by the equipment and infrastructure for transport, unloading and storage that gradually arrived in France from its Atlantic coastline.

As they arrived, twenty-five newly created divisions began to train with the French and nine with the British.

Prior to that, hundreds of French and British instructors travelled to the United States to provide the new recruits with basic military training before they even left for Europe. Throughout this process, however, Pershing and his general staff kept watch to ensure that the French and British instructors did not excessively 'contaminate' American soldiers and officers with their doctrine of trench-to-trench fighting under the protection of heavy artillery, which was seen as incompatible with the young Americans' naturally offensive spirit.

Pershing intended to prepare his troops for a victorious assault on the German positions outside Metz (where his units were gradually stationed from early 1918 as they arrived in France). For him, this offensive in Lorraine was meant to be the prelude to crossing the Rhine and invading Germany at some point in early 1919.

For the French and British general staffs, this date was too distant. They worried about the imminent return of the German troops who had been freed up on the Eastern Front by the collapse of the tsarist regime, followed by that of the Kerensky government and the signing of the peace treaty with the new Bolshevik government in March 1918 at Brest-Litovsk. But Pershing remained inflexible, refusing to make new troops available to the French and British armies. He did agree to one exception, however, making some units consisting of African American soldiers available to the French command. Given the experience of the French command with troops from sub-Saharan Africa (mainly Senegalese infantrymen), and in order partly to respond to the insatiable demand for fresh troops, several units of African American soldiers were actually put under direct French command. Two divisions solely made up of black soldiers – the 92nd and the 93rd – actively took part in the Argonne offensive of the autumn of 1918 in French uniform. They performed very bravely there, what's more, and the three regiments of the 93rd division each received as a whole the French Croix de Guerre for their courage under fire.[70]

# CHAPTER 10

## THE GERMAN SPRING OFFENSIVE OF 1918 AND THE AMERICAN BAPTISM OF FIRE

In early 1918, nearly nine months after the Americans had formally entered the war but six months before they began significantly – and then massively – to contribute to the fighting in material and human terms, the Allies' situation had been seriously eroded. The arrival of American soldiers was awaited with great impatience.

On the Western Front, the French and British armies were morally and physically exhausted. Among the French, the human disaster of the Nivelle offensive (270,000 killed and wounded) at the Chemin des Dames (launched on 16 April 1917) resulted in many episodes of collective disobedience.[71] From that time on, the general staff and its new commander-in-chief, Philippe Pétain, increased leave for soldiers, accelerated troop rotation and temporarily abstained from major new offensive operations in order to address concerns about troop morale.

On the Italian front, the Italians suffered a disaster at Caporetto in October 1917.[72]

On the Eastern Front, the Russian army gradually disintegrated over the course of 1917 with the successive collapse of the tsarist regime and the Kerensky government, the latter of which had attempted to pursue the fight against the Central Powers. But the regime, weak from the start, was in no position to fight simultaneously the Germans, the Austrians, the Turks and the nascent White, Red and various ethnic insurrections (which included Tatars, Ukrainians, Baltic populations and the peoples of the Caucasus) then underway. Desertions increased, constantly weakening the Russian army's fighting ability.

In March 1918, a peace treaty between the Central Powers and the new Bolshevik regime was signed at Brest-Litovsk in modern Belarus. The latter sought to exploit the ongoing civil war to establish its power. In addition to winning significant territorial gains, this allowed the Germans to transfer a large portion of their troops in the east to the Western Front.

In the Middle East, the British troops fighting the Turks in Mesopotamia found themselves bogged down after having taken Baghdad in the spring of 1917. By contrast, the Arab uprising led by the Hashemite dynasty against Turkish domination, with support from T.E. Lawrence and the British, advanced from Arabia to the Near East, capturing Jerusalem in November 1917.

In the Balkans, the landing of Allied troops in Thessaloníki and the involvement of Romania resulted in bloody stalemate. The French troops of the Army of the East who came by way of Thessaloníki suffered heavy casualties, mainly the result of diseases (typhus and various fevers) that slowed, even paralysed their operations.


Conceived by the German general staff, Operation Michael represented a major shift in how the war was conducted.

In early 1918, Ludendorff was convinced that the German army needed to attempt a decisive offensive before massive numbers of American troops began to arrive in France – an eventuality that the failed submarine war now made inevitable – and definitively tipped the strategic scales in favour of the Allies.

In order to resume offensive operations, Ludendorff counted on three factors that he hoped would prove decisive when taken together.

First, the signature in March 1918 of the Treaty of Brest-Litovsk with Russia's newly installed Bolshevik regime freed up fifty divisions from the Eastern Front. These reinforcements gave the Germans a significant human advantage. They could now line up 190 divisions (or around 3.5 million men) against 170 French, British and Belgian ones. As the Germans knew, theirs was a merely temporary advantage: though they would require several months of training, starting in 1918 between 100,000 and 150,000 American soldiers arrived in Europe each month.

Second, the Germans also possessed a unified command structure, unlike the French and British, whose respective strategic choices were not always coordinated.

Third, thanks to the absolute priority given war production in late 1916 (a source of hardship for the civilian population), they had an abundant stock of heavy artillery together with extensive munitions stockpiles.

Finally, Ludendorff wished to make use of an innovative tactic that involved overrunning enemy positions with assault troops rather than massed frontal attack. German generals had noted that, for themselves and their adversaries alike, the massive frontal assault had become ever less effective, even when preceded by long and heavy artillery bombardment. It was precisely this method of attacking that had a year earlier resulted in the French army's catastrophic failure at the Chemin des Dames.

Ludendorff thus decided to entrust the attack to the *Sturmtruppen*, newly created elite units consisting of the best members (whether officers or simple soldiers) selected from existing units.[73] Rather than launching a frontal assault, these soldiers had to infiltrate enemy lines as rapidly as possible, bypass fortified positions and promptly destroy command posts and ammunition dumps. Above all, they had to appear as quickly as they could behind Allied lines and, using the element of surprise, disorganize the enemy's defence in order to provoke a panicked retreat.

The *Sturmtruppen* were to advance following a short but extremely violent artillery preparation that once again targeted command posts and artillery and machine-gun positions rather than the entirety of the enemy line. This new approach had been developed and successfully tested in the east in 1917 against the Russian army, particularly on the Baltic front, and then again in Italy.

Ludendorff chose first and foremost to attack the British army, thinking that, once its morale had been broken, it would possibly set off for the Channel ports, forcing a negotiated peace upon the Allies that would be, at the very least, favourable to Germany. On 21 March 1918, Operation Michael thus began, with the Germans vigorously attacking British positions in Picardy between Arras and La Fère.

In the first days of the offensive, the *Sturmtruppen* moved very rapidly. In forty-eight hours, German soldiers had advanced more than thirty-five kilometres. As British units retreated, they left behind a large number of casualties and enormous quantities of prisoners and materiel.

With the liaison between their respective armies threatened, tensions rapidly appeared between the French and British general staffs. The British wished to defend Amiens, the nerve centre of their system. For the French, however, it was above all a question of defending the approaches to Paris. They thus wished to position their troops closer to the capital.

Faced with this emergency, a very important decision was taken on 28 March 1918: a unified military command for the Allied forces was established that for the first time included American forces. Its command was entrusted to Marshal Foch. After a few days, the British succeeded in organizing an in-depth defence with the help of some French reinforcements. The bulk of German troops (whose units, it should be recalled, had been deprived of their best members) had trouble keeping up with and thereby consolidating the *Sturmtruppen*'s advance. Outside Arras, the British defence stiffened and the confrontation once again began to take the form of a traditional battle of attrition and position. The British had fallen back as much as sixty-five kilometres, lost more than 160,000 men killed or wounded and left more than 60,000 prisoners. But German casualties had also been very heavy. Above all, the front had not been broken once and for all or the British army put to rout. Ludendorff thus called a halt to the offensive in Picardy.

He resumed it almost immediately, once again attacking the British as well as Belgian and Portuguese contingents on 9 April, this time on the river Lys in Flanders and outside Ypres ('Operation Georgette').[74]

Faced with British resistance and the arrival of French reinforcements, the German offensive once again became bogged down after a string of significant early successes. At the end of April, Ludendorff once again suspended the offensive.

He decided now to attack the French army. This was 'Operation Blücher'.[75] He did not anticipate total victory but wished to immobilize and weaken his adversary before turning around and carrying out a final attack, which he hoped would this time prove decisive, against the British.

Ludendorff concentrated on a relatively large front in the

Aisne stretching roughly 100 kilometres from Montdidier to Reims. Launched before dawn on 27 May, the offensive initially focused on a sector between Noyon and Reims.

At 01.00, the Germans unleashed an intense artillery barrage (including mustard-gas shells) against French lines. Three hours later, seventeen German divisions attacked the French front line, held by six divisions. It was an immediate success: one after the other, the French divisions of the Third Army gave way and began to withdraw in disorder. At 11.00, the Germans reached the French second line on the Aisne. That night, they were at the river Vesle, having covered more than fifteen kilometres since leaving their departure trenches (and in doing so achieving one of the most rapid one-day advances since the start of the war). The next day, the Germans entered Soissons. They recaptured the Chemin des Dames and, on 30 May – nearly four years after their first incursion – the German vanguard once again crossed the Marne at Dormans. In four days, the French army had retreated more than forty-five kilometres, leaving behind 650 artillery pieces, 2,000 machine guns and 60,000 prisoners.

This had a disastrous impact on French civilian and military morale. French troops began to pour back to the rear. As in the summer of 1914, the spectacle of their retreat provoked a mass exodus as civilians hastily abandoned their homes, slowing the movement of reinforcements to the front. And, as in September 1914, it seemed that Paris might be threatened, with the government once again considering relocation to Bordeaux. Over the course of the weekend of 1 June, nearly a million Parisians left the city without delay using whatever means were at their disposal.[76]

It was in these dramatic circumstances that the AEF had its true baptism of fire on the French front.

In late May 1918, the American deployment in France continued to advance as the first divisions arrived and their training moved forward.

At this time, the US Army consisted of more than 1.9 million men (most of whom were still in basic training), including nearly 800,000 volunteers. Out of this total, nearly 500,000 had already arrived in France and Great Britain. Their training completed, the AEF now consisted of roughly 300,000 men divided between eleven divisions, most of which were positioned outside Metz and its surroundings. Three additional divisions were about to set sail for Europe.[77] The expeditionary corps was thus already a significant force, though it was still neither fully operational nor battle-tested as an autonomous army manoeuvring with its own command and logistics structure.

Ready or not, the German offensive of 27 May offered to plunge the soldiers of the AEF directly into the extraordinarily intense type of battle that had developed over the course of the conflict. They did so with a determination that impressed their allies and, above all, their adversaries.

In truth, it had been decided before the onset of Operation Michael to engage at least one US Army division. This was the US 1st Infantry Division, which from early May had been stationed outside the little village of Cantigny a few kilometres to the west of Montdidier in the Somme.

Even before the German offensive, 28 May had been selected for the first attack to be conducted by a full American unit. That day, the 1st Division was to attack Cantigny, the location of which constituted a salient jutting into Allied lines. Despite the onset of the German offensive on the morning of the 27th 100 kilometres to the south-east, the Allied command maintained the American order to attack. In purely military terms, Cantigny was not a very significant objective. Having been taken and retaken by French and German forces over the course of the preceding months, it was little more than a rubble heap. But for Pershing and General Robert Lee Bullard, commander of the 1st Division, it was an important test of American troops' ability to manoeuvre in battle formation;

hitherto, their participation had been mainly confined to surprise attacks conducted by small units. It thus represented an opportunity to test how well US soldiers could not just conquer a given objective, but also defend against the inevitable German counter-attacks. In support of the American attack, the French allocated significant resources in artillery and aeroplanes.

The attack launched by American soldiers at 06.45 after a (relatively short) one-hour preliminary bombardment rapidly resulted in the village's capture and this without huge casualties. Once the objective had been achieved, however, defending this new position proved a difficult task. For the planned air support was immediately withdrawn, as were the artillery and tanks supplied by the French army – all resources now needed to defend against the German offensive now underway. In an effort to recapture Cantigny, Germans fiercely counter-attacked with fresh units late in the afternoon. Ferocious and confused fighting ensued for the rest of the night and the following day. Only a final charge led by the former president's son, Major Theodore Roosevelt, allowed the Germans to be repelled. During the night of 29 May, the latter gave up their attacks, leaving the American soldiers in control of the pile of rubble that had been the village of Cantigny.

In strategic terms, it was a relatively minor event, one that took place at a remove from the main battlefield to the southeast. In tactical terms, by contrast, the engagement proved very important for the American, French and also German general staffs: for the first time in this conflict, a US division had gone into battle on its own, achieved its objectives and proved itself capable of holding the conquered positions against fierce and repeated German attack.

This supplied Pershing and the Allied generals with solid grounds for confidence as to the fighting capacity of American soldiers when facing the Germany army. Ready or not, the American forces would soon have to fight.

The arrival on the battlefield of the 2nd Division of the AEF took place in a context reminiscent of Dante. It was originally planned for the American 2nd Division to relieve the 1st at Cantigny, but the success of the German offensive north of Reims and its drive towards the Marne completely changed the situation. The Germans now threatened Château-Thierry, their vanguard just seventy kilometres from Paris. The capital was, moreover, receiving fire from several very long-range German howitzers – known as 'Big Berthas' – that had been stationed in the Oise.[78] A pall hung over the Allied general staffs. At the last moment and after much hesitation, it was thus decided to send the US 2nd Division to a position adjoining the village of Veaux and facing a forest known as Belleau Wood, slightly to the east of Château-Thierry.

On the night of 31 May, the American troops were first transported by train from their positions in Lorraine to the station of Meaux in Seine-et-Marne. Over the course of the night, the four regiments that composed the 2nd Division (the 9th and 23rd Infantry Regiments as well as the 5th and 6th Marine Regiments) attempted to reach the positions assigned them via a series of marches and counter-marches that reflected the hesitation of French generals. Their progress along the roads was slowed by the flow of civilians headed the other way to escape the fighting as well as by retreating – indeed, already routed – French soldiers. One marine recounted his march towards the battlefield, the artillery rumbling in the distance:

> No man who saw that road in the first days of June ever forgot it. A stream of old men and children and old and young women turned out of their homes between two sunrises, with what they could carry in their hands [...] women carrying babies. Children – solemn little

boys in black pinafores and curly-headed, high-nosed little girls, trudging hand-in-hand. People of elegance and refinement in inadequate shoes. Broad-faced peasants. Inhabitants of a thousand peaceful little villages and farms, untouched by the war since 1914. Now the Boche was out again [...] There were French soldiers in the rout, too. Nearly all were wounded or in the last stages of exhaustion. They did not appear to be first-line troops; they were old, bearded fellows of forty and fifty-five, territorials or mean, unpleasant-looking Algerians, such troops as are put in to hold a quiet sector.[79]

Finally, after yet further exhausting marches, the US Marines arrived in the little village of Lucy-le-Bocage at nightfall, where their commander, Brigadier General James C. Harbord, had just set up his headquarters. They did not eat or ate little. They did not know where they were. They were – literally – in the dark.

For the first time, they would be obliged to fight the German army as it hurled towards Paris and their commander decided that they should immediately attack it head on. One might have thought that troops exhausted and disorganized after being constantly on the move for seventy-two hours in forced marches would be given time to get organized, resupply and prepare defensive positions. But no. At the request of General Degoutte, French Sixth Army commander, and with the enthusiastic support of Pershing himself, it was decided to attack immediately without reconnaissance or preparation. The soldiers of the US 2nd Division were to pay for this choice in flesh and blood.

# CHAPTER 11

## WHAT WAS THE TRUE MILITARY IMPACT OF THE BATTLE OF BELLEAU WOOD?

It is a striking fact that the perception of the fighting that began on 6 June 1918 and continued until 25 June has widely varied from one vantage point and period to the next. For purposes of simplicity, two extremes may be identified:

- an American view deeply anchored in the historiography of the Marine Corps, according to which, by blunting the spearhead of the German advance, the fighting allowed the Allies to prevent a withdrawal from being transformed into a rout, a German breakthrough towards Paris and likely defeat, thus ultimately setting the stage for their victory five months later;
- the view of a portion of the French general staff who, even as they hailed the fighting spirit of the American soldier, attributed no more than symbolic value to the confused

and bloody fray that took place over more than two weeks in this little wood.

At the archives of France's Defence Historical Service, it is always useful to consult the monumental, 22,000-page survey drafted by the French War Ministry in the early 1920s.[80] Written by staff officers who had a few years earlier witnessed the fighting they describe, it supplies an interesting indication – in point of the number of pages they devote to it – of the significance of the contributions made by the various allies as they were perceived by the French side.

The French vision of the events is instructive: of the five pages devoted to summarizing the fighting of 6 June 1918, across the length of the front, just one part of one sentence – no more than a single line of text – is devoted to the fighting in Belleau Wood: 'while the American 2nd Division succeeded in taking a portion of Belleau Wood and repulsing an attack'.[81] That's all.

As is often the case, dispassionate analysis lends itself to a judgement halfway between these extremes. The French army did in fact find itself in a difficult situation in early June. Launched on 28 May, Operation Blücher was the third German offensive of their spring campaign but the first to target the French army directly. It took the general staff by surprise as they had not expected a direct attack, above all not in Champagne. Their best units were not stationed there and they retreated in shock. After several days, the first German troops reached the Marne – an important success in military, symbolic and psychological terms. For the first time since September 1914, Paris came under German artillery fire.

The part played by the American press in foregrounding the role of the US Marines is also a matter of debate. The army has always taken pains to maintain a positive image with the population in order to ensure that it has the support of public opinion, particularly in its dealings with Congress.

It was generally acknowledged in France at that time that the nation had the right to demand the ultimate sacrifice from its children in order to defend itself. This was not necessarily the case in the United States, particularly when the demand came from the distant federal government.

Keen to retain the favour of public opinion, the AEF was thus more inclined than the Allied armies to allow journalists to be present and even to closely follow operations. The particular details that these correspondents could cite in drafting their articles were generally subject to fairly rigorous restrictions. In particular, regulations prohibited them from specifically referring by name to a military unit in a given location, though they were allowed to refer generically to the 'ground army'. In 1918, American war correspondents in France received permission to treat the Marine Corps as a military branch distinct from the US Army. Beginning on 6 June 1918, the *Chicago Tribune* was thus able to run front-page stories written by its star correspondent, Floyd Gibbons, on the US Marines' exploits at Belleau Wood. That allowed the American press, fourteen months after Congress recognized 'a state of war with Germany', finally to report – in heroic and favourable terms, what's more – that American troops had begun to participate massively in the European conflict.

This was indisputably a public-relations godsend for the Marine Corps. To the great displeasure of the US Army's leaders, particularly those of the 2nd Infantry Division to which the US Marine brigade was attached, Marine Corps press officers presented the role played by their soldiers in a way that almost completely excluded that of other infantry units.

For the US Marines, in fact, the positive effect was almost immediate: on 9 June, the *New York Times* reported that the number of volunteers presenting themselves at US Marine recruitment offices had doubled following the reports on their 'triumph' at Belleau Wood. On 1 July Congress, until then sceptical as to the virtues of the Marine Corps's very existence, voted to fund its expansion from 15,000 to 75,000 men.[82] Henceforth, the existence of the Marine Corps as an independent branch of the American armed forces was reinforced, no doubt once and for all. Conversely, the other branches of the armed forces grew deeply resentful of what they saw as a semi-intentional effort to overshadow them – a source of resentment that to some degree continues to this day.

Who thus really stopped the German offensive launched on 28 May? The fact is that, when the marines attacked Belleau Wood at dawn on 6 June, Operation Blücher had already run out of steam. As in earlier offensives, the better part of the German troops – exhausted and undermanned due to the ravages of Spanish influenza – found it difficult to keep up with the *Sturmtruppen*. The fighting in which American troops participated in the first days of June – particularly outside Château-Thierry – had already significantly slowed the German advance. This is why the German command, which had already begun preparations for the next offensive (Operation Georgette on 10 June), sought to establish a fundamentally defensive position in Belleau Wood.

In this sense, the American attack on 6 June did not 'save Paris'. Given the wood's strategic importance, however, it did have a disproportionate influence on the remainder of the conflict. By choosing to hold the position at all costs and even reinforcing it at the detriment of the upcoming offensive, the German general staff made the battle a test of the relative value of the German and American armies. If the Americans had ultimately failed to take the wood or even needed to be propped up or replaced by French troops, the result would have been to give the German army a sort of psychological upper hand, reassuring troops worried about the appearance of massive numbers of doughboys across from them.

Yet despite their many operational shortcomings, the tactical weakness of their command and the casualties they suffered, the aggressiveness of the American troops established that the US Army was a formidable opponent, not just in the eyes of the German command but above all in those of its troops.

# CHAPTER 12

## THE LAST HUNDRED DAYS OF THE WAR

### THE SECOND BATTLE OF THE MARNE

It was in September 1918 that Pershing began to achieve his personal strategic objective: to command an American army that, while obviously cooperating with those of its allies, had its own resources and above all an autonomous command – his.

Despite the resistance of Foch, who was sceptical as to the tactical skills of American generals, and that of the French premier Georges Clemenceau, who was above all impatient to see as many American soldiers as possible join the fighting, Pershing gradually acquired responsibility for an entire section of the front. He was helped in this by the discreet but effective support of General Pétain, commander of the French army and hardly an admirer of Foch.

It was at this point that the conflict turned, shifting from a long period of defence against the successive German offensives that began in March to the start of the final Allied advance. The enemy had been weakened. But though it was increasingly demoralized about its chances for victory, it was still effective and determined in what gradually became a fight to defend German territory.

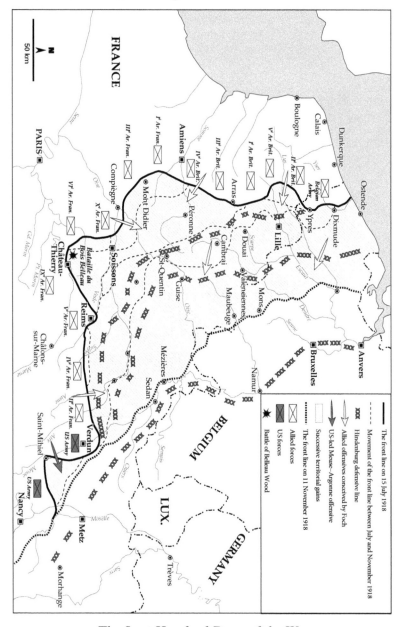

*The Last Hundred Days of the War*

The *Friedensturm* represented the last German attempt at a decisive offensive: in early July 1918, Ludendorff became convinced that time was now against him. Nearly a million American soldiers had already reached Europe, even if many of them were far from ready to be sent to the front. The situation of the German units facing them was increasingly critical. Despite the absolute priority that had been given to war production since the preceding summer, German soldiers began to lack for many things, particularly in terms of supply. Moreover, it became increasingly difficult to make up for casualties in fighting units. In addition to those wounded or killed in the incessant fighting that had taken place since late March, the Spanish-flu epidemic devastated the German ranks and disrupted many units.

Ludendorff thus brought together all available forces. Indeed, he went further, calling up the class of 1920 in advance and immediately dispatching to the front German soldiers who had been taken prisoner by the Russians and only just been freed.

Baptized *Friedensturm* ('peace offensive'), this final push began at dawn on 15 July between Soissons and Château-Thierry. With the Kaiser present at the front, around forty German divisions hurled themselves against French positions. Their objective was to reach the Marne once again and, this time, to break through in the direction of Paris.

Thanks to documents recuperated in the course of a successful raid carried out the night before, the French commander was aware of the location and imminence of the German attack.[83] The general staff implemented a tactical innovation initiated by Pétain: they chose to withdraw most of their front-line troops and artillery to the rear. The German attack thus fell upon a vacuum but came up against a very well-defended second line, its hitherto silent artillery intact. The German offensive gradually became bogged down.

On 18 July, the Allied troops launched a counter-attack. General Charles Mangin's Tenth Army and General Degoutte's Sixth Army (with its contingent of American divisions) went into battle. After very heavy fighting, the US 2nd Division, which had won fame at Belleau Wood, recaptured Château-Thierry, held since June by the Germans, who were forced to retreat, albeit in good order and while inflicting heavy casualties on their adversaries.

In addition to the American troops' now numerically significant impact, the mid-July fighting was marked by the decisive intervention of a large number of Renault light tanks, the first model to be equipped with a mobile turret. This tank proved more effective than the heavy models that had gone before them, starting in 1916. This is also when the Allies achieved decisive air superiority. Beyond the real numerical advantage they enjoyed, the tactical use of aerial forces to supply coordinated ground support for infantry became increasingly precise and sophisticated.

This fighting subsequently became known as the Second Battle of the Marne. Its success won Foch the baton of a Marshal of France. It also won the US 1st Army Corps a citation on the part of the army. Drafted by General Mangin, the citation read:

> Shoulder to shoulder with your French comrades, you were thrown into the counter-offensive battle which commenced on the 18th of July. You rushed into the fight as though to a fete […] You have shown yourselves worthy Sons of your Great Country and you were admired by your brothers in arms […] American Comrades! I am grateful to you for the blood so generously spilled on the soil of my country.[84]

On 8 August 1918, an Anglo-French army successfully attacked in Picardy, advancing roughly ten kilometres. Even though this advance was ultimately stopped by the Germans, from this point on Ludendorff himself despaired of final victory.[85] He submitted his resignation to the Kaiser, who refused to accept it.

## THE MEUSE-ARGONNE OFFENSIVE

With additional American soldiers constantly arriving, in August 1918 Foch in his turn felt that he could prepare a series of attacks against a German army now on the defensive. In this context, Pershing made preparations to reduce the Saint-Mihiel 'salient', an inverted triangle south-east of Verdun, leading the first offensive planned and developed by the AEF in France.

It almost never took place: on 30 August, Foch travelled to Pershing's headquarters to present his new plans. Given recent British successes in Picardy, rather than a series of distinct attacks on the part of the various Allied armies, Foch now planned for one vast operation to catch the German army in a pincer movement and thereby encircle it.

In this context, a specific attack on Saint-Mihiel was no longer useful. The US Army would find itself split in half, arrayed along the two wings of the French army, and – a final insult – French generals would be assigned to 'assist' their American counterparts.

This was unacceptable to Pershing. Unsurprisingly, the interview between the two men turned sour. Foch went so far as to ask him if he really wanted to fight.[86]

In the debate that followed, which took a political turn, Pershing was often supported by Pétain as well as (more surprisingly) Clemenceau, who was concerned to avoid excessively annoying the great American ally.

Finally, on 2 September, it was decided that the US Army on its own would take responsibility for the portion of the front between Pont-à-Mousson in Lorraine and the Argonne forest, and that it would begin reducing the Saint-Mihiel salient on 10 September. Then, beginning on the 30th, it would join a great general offensive of the Allied forces in the direction of Belgium.

For the American commander, the question now was to prove in the field not just that he was at the head of brave soldiers, but also that he was capable of managing complex operations, of coordinating the movements of great masses of men and many units – something of which the French generals were clearly far from convinced.

Following an intense artillery preparation, on the morning of 12 September three US Army corps, reinforced by a French army corps (for a total of 200,000 and 50,000 men, respectively), attacked the point and sides of the triangle that formed the salient. The 80,000 Germans responsible for defending it understood that they were going to be overrun, and began rapidly to evacuate the salient, protected by the fierce resistance of their front-line troops. The Americans reached their objectives in less than twenty-four hours, taking a large number of prisoners. Most of the German soldiers were nevertheless able to withdraw. Despite this mixed result and many tactical and logistical mistakes, the operation was nevertheless presented to the public as an American success and hailed as such, particularly by the Allied press.[87]

The Meuse-Argonne offensive of the autumn of 1918 crowned America's participation in the final phase of the war. As Pershing had wished, his troops took part as an army under American command reporting to Supreme Allied

Commander Foch – at parity with Pétain for the French army and Field Marshal Douglas Haig for the British.

The attack began on 26 September and lasted forty-seven days. At the outset of the operation, the Allies advanced rather rapidly, but the German defence soon stiffened considerably. Although some exhausted and demoralized units began to disintegrate behind the front, German front-line soldiers continued to fight with determination. At stake now was access to the Rhine and the possibility that the fighting would continue on the soil of Germany itself. Their experience of the four previous years led them to do all they could to save their country and loved ones from such a trial.

Moreover, the terrain – the forests of the Argonne, for example – lent itself very well to defensive combat, especially given the fact that the German general staff had long before established several lines there. Known as the Hindenburg and Stella Freyung lines, they consisted of networks of fortified strongpoints and concrete blockhouses. It was on these positions that the German resistance focused.

In fact, the Allied troops' advance in the last weeks of the war was accompanied by heavy losses. On a front that extended from Verdun to south of the forests of the Argonne, the Americans lost 120,000 men (22,000 of whom were killed in November) – more than 2,000 dead per day. US Army logistics often left something to be desired, much like that of the French and British armies early in the war. The logistics of an army advancing under enemy fire lent themselves no more to improvisation than did commanding men under fire in unprecedented circumstances. The American general staff learned this the hard way and the soldiers under their command paid for this apprenticeship with their blood. On 11 November, they finally reached their objective, pushing the Germans back to the other side of the Meuse. The final days of the war witnessed what was almost a race between the American 1st and 2nd divisions to seize the symbolic town of Sedan before French troops could do so.[88]

It was in the final weeks of the war – specifically, on 8 October 1918 – that soldier Alvin Callum York performed his feat of arms. In the United States, it would become something of an archetype in the representation of combat in the First World War.

Born into a family of poor white farmers in the mountains of Tennessee, the deeply religious York initially sought recognition as a conscientious objector on the basis of his religious faith. He was nevertheless drafted and, during his training in the United States, became convinced that God wished him to fight in Europe. He thus decided to become an exemplary soldier.

On 8 October, York was on patrol behind German lines with a group of fifteen men. Falling into an ambush, they came under German machine-gun fire, which inflicted heavy casualties on the group. While his comrades took cover, York returned fire on his adversaries. With his rifle and pistol, he alone killed twenty-eight of them and took the others prisoner. He then returned to the American lines with his catch: 132 Germans, four of whom were officers.

Though of no real importance in the field, this episode nevertheless immediately supplied a template for American media reporting on the war. It offered an ideal vision of the US soldier as seen by Pershing: 'A young American and his rifle'. Alvin York was immediately made a sergeant and received the Distinguished Service Cross as well as the French Croix de Guerre. But that was only the start of what became an avalanche of distinctions: within a month, he would be the most decorated American soldier of the war. Following his triumphant return to the United States, his war journal was adapted as an autobiography and in the 1920s became a bestseller.

In 1940, a new conflict was approaching for the United States, though isolationist sentiment remained very strong there. For Hollywood, the time had come to remobilize the country. Warner Brothers seized upon York's story and, in 1941, Howard Hawks's film *Sergeant York* was released, with the charismatic Gary Cooper in the title role. It was an immediate success.

# CHAPTER 13

## AFTER THE ARMISTICE, THEN THE TREATY OF VERSAILLES

Given the deteriorating material and health conditions of the German army, in early October 1918 the nation's military and political leadership realized that it would soon no longer be capable of stopping the Allied armies. Eventually, German territory would be invaded.

They thus sought to initiate peace talks before the German army collapsed and was obliged purely and simply to surrender. Knowing that the French and British would seek to impose extremely harsh terms, they thus decided to turn to the United States, hoping that it would be capable of convincing its allies to accept more moderate armistice clauses.

In a speech before Congress on 8 January that – in Germany as elsewhere – caused a considerable stir, Wilson had laid out the country's war aims in fourteen points. The president's objective was nothing less than the fundamental transformation of relations between the nations of the world.[89]

On 6 October 1918, the US State Department received by way of Switzerland a German note asking after the conditions for an armistice based on the fourteen points.

The Americans consulted their French and British allies, who demanded that any cessation of hostilities take place in such a way that Germany would not later be able to resume the fight. Foch, in particular, made it a condition of any armistice that the German army withdraw beyond the Rhine, abandoning on site the better part of its materiel, in particular its artillery. The British, for their part, insisted that German naval capacity be immediately dismantled. Pershing, finally, was sceptical as to the durability of any cessation of hostilities that had not been preceded by the decisive defeat of the German army. It was his personal ambition, it should be recalled, to lead the US Army to victory on the other side of the Rhine in spring 1919…

On 14 October, a note summarizing the Allied demands was sent to Berlin. Things then accelerated on the German side under the twofold pressure of the deteriorating situation on the Western Front and, above all, the country's gradual abandonment by its allies. The Austrians, in particular, signed a separate armistice with the Italians. On 20 October, the new German chancellor, Prince Max von Baden, accepted the principle of Allied conditions. On 27 October, Ludendorff, who ultimately favoured continuing the fight, resigned from his post as quartermaster general of the German army (his official title) under pressure from Max von Baden.

Finally, on 9 November, Wilhelm II abandoned his throne and went into exile in the Netherlands.[90] Simultaneously, Max von Baden resigned and called upon Friedrich Ebert, the leader of the German Social Democrats (the largest parliamentary group in the Reichstag), to head the government. German plenipotentiaries appeared at the French outposts on 7 November, and the Armistice was signed in keeping with the Allies' conditions on the night of 10–11 November.

It took effect at eleven o'clock on the morning of the next day, 11 November, the 1,562nd day of the war.

In the mind of the Democrat Wilson, the United States had mainly entered the war to secure a major role at the discussion table regarding the definition of a new world order. The discussions leading up to the Treaty of Versailles and the creation of the League of Nations precisely corresponded to his objectives. The American population, however, did not share his enthusiasm. The elections of 5 November 1918 brought a Republican majority to both the Senate and the House of Representatives – a reflection of the weariness of American public opinion, if not its disavowal of Wilsonian policy. Wilson nevertheless decided to involve himself directly and maximally in negotiations relating to the forthcoming peace. This was because, beyond the American contribution to military victory, his personal objective – in keeping with the philosophy of the professor of political science he had always been – was to bring about a fundamental transformation of international relations.

He thus personally led his delegation at the Paris discussions, making him the first president of the United States to travel abroad on an official trip. And he was away for long periods (more than three months over two trips), a cause for surprise – and shock – in Washington.

It is true that the discussions that took place in Paris from January 1919 were extremely difficult. They brought together the representatives of thirty-two nations and nationalities as well as thousands of experts (including 1,300 for the American delegation alone). The sessions of the plenary discussions were public but in fact all decisions were taken privately between the leaders of the United States (Wilson), France (Clemenceau), Britain (David Lloyd George) and Italy (Vittorio Emanuele Orlando), who met nearly 150 times. Given the impressive number of subjects to be covered and choices to be made, the pressure on the negotiators – temporal and otherwise – was extreme.

With mixed results, Wilson strove to make his fourteen points the basis of negotiations and establish the League of Nations so dear to him. This ran counter to the Franco-British desire to lay blame for the conflict solely on Germany. Beyond its symbolic aspect, doing so would pave the way for imposing steep reparations on the defeated party. The French absolutely counted on this to finance the reconstruction of the northern quarter of the country, which had been devastated by four years of fighting. For their part, the British, whose territory had been spared, counted on reparations to finance pensions for veterans, war widows and orphans and re-establish the position of the pound sterling, which before the conflict had been the world's dominant currency.

The other subject that presented multiple stumbling blocks concerned the fixing of post-war borders – and not just in Europe. Once again, Wilsonian idealism found itself confronted, among other things, with the existence of secret treaties concluded between certain allies over the course of the conflict. Such was the case, for example, with the 1916 Sykes–Picot Accord (named after its French and British negotiators), which defined new borders and the zones of French and British protectorates in the Near East.

Eager to avoid creating a new Alsace-Lorraine, in Europe Wilson opposed Clemenceau's wish to deprive Germany of sovereignty over the left bank of the Rhine. To compensate for this and reassure the French, he proposed that a joint defensive treaty be signed between the French, British and Americans. Wilson grew increasingly fatigued and his health began to fail.

What's more, he had to fight hard to ensure that the creation of the League of Nations be made an integral part of the future peace treaty. Having finally obtained satisfaction on this point, over the course of the last weeks of discussions he adopted a relatively hard stance with German negotiators, who argued – not without reason – that the result was a text far removed from the spirit of Wilson's fourteen-points speech.

On 28 June 1919, the Treaty of Versailles was solemnly signed in the Hall of Mirrors.[91] Wilson left the next day for the United States.


Upon his return to Washington, he first of all occupied himself with getting the treaty ratified by the Senate. Doing so proved difficult from the outset.

Republicans now held a majority in both chambers and many congressmen were openly isolationist, particularly those from the country's south and west. Hostile to any formal engagement on the part of the United States in the context of a collective security mechanism, they were convinced that relations between European nations were fundamentally conflictual and that the treaty would inevitably drag the United States into endless military expeditions abroad. Indeed, the terms of the debate regarding the conditions and possible circumstances for engaging American troops outside the country have evolved remarkably little over the past hundred years.

The key position of chairman of the Senate Foreign Relations Committee was held by Henry Cabot Lodge, a Republican senator from Massachusetts. Lodge was open to voting in favour of the treaty on condition that it be modified and adjusted in a number of ways.

Authoritarian, always brittle and also very tired, Wilson dug his heels in. His health declining, in early September he set out on a rail tour of the American Midwest and West Coast to win over public opinion.[92] But it was beginning to turn against him. The economic and political situation of the country was rapidly deteriorating. The soldiers' (relatively rapid) return from Europe and the cessation of military orders and price controls brought a combination of higher unemployment, economic slowdown and inflation. The number of labour strikes increased in 1920 and they were accompanied by growing political agitation, the distant echo of European turmoil associated with the Bolsheviks' success in Russia.

Popular attitudes towards immigration considerably hardened. Concerns over job competition became mixed with fears relating to the contaminating influence of political radicalism, mainly originating in central and Eastern Europe.[93]

Worried, the French and British ambassadors to Washington strove to facilitate compromise between the Senate majority and the president.

Weary, the latter finally suffered a stroke on 27 September that left him between life and death for several days. Partially paralysed, cloistered away by his wife and doctors, Wilson's attitude now became inflexible.

On 19 November, a clear majority of the US Senate (fifty-five votes against thirty-nine) for the first time rejected ratification of the Treaty of Versailles. In the wake of this vote, a compromise text was prepared by Lodge and submitted to a new vote in March 1920. Once again, a combination of determined isolationists and some of Wilson's dogmatic partisans brought about its defeat – this time, definitively – by blocking any possible membership in the League of Nations he had created. The proposed military guarantees to France were not even submitted to a vote.

Woodrow Wilson briefly toyed with the idea of making the November 1920 presidential election a sort of referendum on the peace conditions. But his state of health prevented him from running and, in 1924, he died. The Republican William Harding, the self-proclaimed candidate of a 'return to normalcy', very handsomely defeated his Democratic opponent, James Cox, with 16 million votes against Cox's 9 million. The following year, Harding, eager to bring this episode of US international engagement formally to a close, had the Senate adopt separate peace treaties with Germany, Austria and a now independent Hungary. The Senate's failure to ratify the treaty marked a profound and long-lasting retreat on the part of the United States from all constraining forms of international involvement.

The international role of the United States significantly declined over the course of the next twenty years. With the attention of the entire society now focused on internal questions, public opinion favoured a complete and rapid end to the war.

# CHAPTER 14

## WAR'S END FOR THE UNITED STATES

It is striking to note just how fast and thoroughly American public opinion and society reverted to isolationist positions at war's end, giving the country's involvement in the conflict between 1917 and 1918 the appearance of a brief parenthesis. Once the exceptional circumstances produced by the audacity of Germany's leaders and the ideological voluntarism of Woodrow Wilson had dissipated, America as a whole hastened to the turn the page on an adventure that many in retrospect saw as too costly in human and material terms as well as politically unproductive. Twenty years later, this would profoundly affect the conditions under which the United States entered a new global conflict.

The repatriation of American troops took place as quickly as possible: altogether, a little more than 2 million American soldiers disembarked in France over the course of the conflict. As is typical of a modern army, in which logistics and services occupy a major place, only two thirds of them spent time at the front, with the rest being entirely assigned to logistical, medical or administrative tasks behind the lines.

From the time when the US 1st Division first tossed its hat into the ring at Cantigny on 25 April until the Armistice, the US Army was on campaign for 200 days. These included forty-seven days following the start of the Battle of Meuse–Argonne when it operated at army rather than divisional strength. In October 1918, the AEF held nearly a quarter of the front line, or more than the British army at the same time.[94]

After the Armistice was signed but before any peace treaty had been, American troops in France carried out a twofold movement. For the great majority of soldiers, this was the start of their demobilization and return to the United States. This process began rather rapidly on 16 November, even though the signature of a peace treaty between the warring parties was still a very distant prospect. Indeed, given the failure to ratify the Treaty of Versailles, it would not be until 1921 that the war between the United States and Germany formally ended. By 1 May 1919, in any case, 1.9 million American soldiers had been demobilized.

On the other hand, several American divisions participated in the occupation of the left bank of the Rhine. By late 1919, there were five such divisions, or a total of 20,000 men. It would not be until January 1923 that the last American soldiers left Europe.

It is interesting to note that the troops stationed in Germany generally held a rather favourable impression of their time there. American soldiers were struck by the cordial reception they received from the German population and a form of territorial organization that reminded them of the Midwest. It is true that German territory had not been subjected to the war's ravages. Given the rapid collapse of the German currency, the purchasing power of American soldiers was also much greater there than it had been in France. On their return to the United States, this re-evaluation of the erstwhile German enemy had a not insignificant impact on a posteriori perceptions of the validity of US involvement in the conflict and the sacrifices it had entailed.

In the United States, those returning to the country were received in moderately enthusiastic and generous fashion. Once they arrived on American soil but before their demobilization, each American soldier received the following services and gifts:

- an (obligatory) medical check-up;
- his uniform;
- a greatcoat or raincoat;
- sixty dollars;
- a unit of life insurance;
- (for those who served in Europe) his helmet and gas mask (as a souvenir).[95]

It was only once they had returned to their place of origin that the doughboys received a warm welcome in the form of a parade or reception organized by the local authorities. Following this, they found themselves largely left to their own devices to resume the course of their individual and professional lives following roughly a two-year hiatus. Compared to those of their cohort who had not served in the army, which was the majority, they generally lagged behind in all domains. In professional and academic careers, their service was seen as a handicap. After the Second World War, American legislation took a much more innovative path with the establishment of the 'GI Bill', which, by financing veterans' training and university studies, was one source of the post-war prosperity of the American middle class. The case of those who returned home wounded or with a visible disability was of course different in principle but pensions were from the outset very slight and would remain so (100 dollars per month for a 100 per cent handicap, for example). The provisions made to honour the memory of those who did not return were less emotional than in Europe, despite what were nevertheless significant losses, particularly given the short duration during which American troops were in battle.

For, at first glance, the total number of American military casualties over the course of the conflict seems limited, particularly in comparison with that suffered by their allies. For example, where the French army counted roughly 1.4 million dead out of 8 million mobilized, the US Army lost more than 110,000 soldiers, including around 50,000 in combat, out of the 4 million it had mobilized.

The higher proportion of death by illness resulted from the fact that American involvement coincided with the brief but extraordinarily deadly appearance of the Spanish flu between 1917 and 1919.[96]

The 50,000 killed in action may seem a very low figure compared with French losses. Yet this comparison should be put into context by taking into account a number of factors. In a given mode of combat, the total number of casualties is more or less a reflection of the total number of troops exposed to fire and the duration of their presence at the front. The logistics (railroads, in particular) and the combination of compulsory military service (then set at three years), reserve system and the mobilization of former conscripts meant that, in August 1914, the French army was able to send more than 2 million men into battle two weeks after the outbreak of hostilities. For more than four years, the French army would then hold the better part of the Western Front against the German army. The United States officially entered the war in April

1917. But while the first (symbolic) American detachments began to disembark at French ports on the Atlantic coast in the summer of 1917, it was only in late May 1918 that US troops were ready (or sometimes forced) to participate in fighting at the divisional level. This relatively short period during which they were heavily involved in the fighting was nevertheless extremely deadly for the American soldiers who were actually sent into battle – that is, around half of the 2 million men who crossed the Atlantic. This had a significant impact on the a posteriori perception of the conflict within the American population.

The lasting return to isolationism began as soon as the Armistice was announced: over time, the population's attitude towards participation in the conflict and, above all, the decision to dispatch an expeditionary force significantly deteriorated. Local incidents notwithstanding, the census and conscription operations of 1917 were undeniably successes. Following the Armistice and the return of the first soldiers, however, American public opinion quickly grew disenchanted. The rejection of the Treaty of Versailles was just one sign among others that the nation's attention was now once again focused on domestic issues.

This isolationist current continued to predominate in the country in the 1930s, benefiting from the convergence of conservatives, who were eager to prevent the American ideal from being 'contaminated' by fascist and communist forms of collectivism, and liberals, who were eager to conserve the resources necessary for new social transfers and economic stimulus plans. It was a widely shared view among the American public that the European continent was naturally prone to war by its nature and history, and that the United States must absolutely keep out of any mechanism (including that entailed by participation in the League of

Nations) that would automatically involve it in the inevitable conflicts of the future.[97]

As in August 1914, the onset of the war in Europe with the entry of German troops into Poland in September 1939 did not immediately pull the United States into the conflict – far from it. Indeed, the majority of the population clearly favoured neutrality at the time. While the European democracies and Great Britain, in particular, were more favourably perceived than the Axis powers – as had also been the case in 1914 – the latter were not without sympathizers. An openly pro-Nazi organization, the German American Bund, had even been firmly established in the Midwest since the 1930s. Created in early 1940 on the campus of Yale University, an 'America First' committee brought together the various isolationist currents and pursued a very intense propaganda campaign against entering the conflict that had just broken out in Europe. Its main spokesman, the aviator Charles Lindbergh, was immensely influential in the country.

At the time, legislation on the export of arms and other materiel to the warring countries was very restrictive. It basically placed an embargo on deliveries to the warring powers. Under the (prudent) influence of Franklin Delano Roosevelt, certain adjustments were gradually made following the war's outbreak in Europe and Roosevelt's re-election in 1940.[98] The gradual shift to the British side as well as the extension of the 'Lend-Lease' law to the Soviet Union following the start of the German invasion in August 1941 did not for all that lead the United States to enter the war against the Axis powers.[99] Doubting that he enjoyed sufficient support, this was not a risk that Roosevelt was willing to take, even after he was elected for the third time (an unprecedented feat).

It would take the Japanese raid on Pearl Harbor on 7

December 1941 – that is, a direct and planned attack on American territory and against its armed forces – finally to plunge the country into the war. On 8 December, Roosevelt would in his turn recognize a state of war between the United States and Japan. Four days later, Germany and Italy declared war on the United States.[100]

Once again, it would be necessary to recruit, equip, train and send American soldiers to fight in France...

# POST-MORTEM

## RETURNING TO BELLEAU WOOD

The visitor who, on this April day, heads south-west from Château-Thierry towards Belleau Wood travels over hilly terrain that, like a century ago, is almost exclusively devoted to agricultural uses. The road snakes over a chequerboard of colourful fields (green for alfalfa, ochre for wheat, blazing yellow for rapeseed) whose rectangles follow the undulating relief of the terrain. Apart from a few farms, there are not many houses in this region, which forms the frontier between Champagne and the Paris Basin.

The road runs along but does not enter Belleau Wood. Located on a hill, the wood is between 150 and 300 metres from the road – the US Marines' starting position on 6 June 1918. Lightly sloping to the foot of the hill, the ground is regular and without obstacles. From the outset, the men who set off walking that morning must have been fully visible to the German defenders entrenched along the inner edge of the wood, even if those present on that early June day reported that the grain – it had been sowed in this area, hitherto spared the fighting – was already high.

Once the Germans opened fire, it was clear that the attackers were confronted with an unavoidable choice: either rush back in disorder behind the road or, to the contrary, rush forward towards the woods. Under the impetus of those of their officers and NCOs who were not immediately cut down by the first hail of bullets, the marines opted for the second.

Once in the woods, the landscape completely changed. The light, first of all. The vegetation is dense on this spring day, as it must have been in June 1918, the near absence of preliminary bombardment having left the canopy nearly intact. After one has proceeded around ten metres, everything becomes darker and the eye takes some time to adapt to the shadowy light. There was obviously no longer any question of advancing in line formation. Henceforth, the men fought in little groups, out of touch with their comrades walking thirty metres to their left or right. Upon entering the wood, the slope becomes rather steep; one moves forward slowly along little narrow paths snaking between the trees. Since they were unable to see, coordination between the various units was impossible. Within a group, it depended on observing the movements of the officer, NCO or simple soldier who had decided to take the initiative and lead his comrades forward.

After 200 or 300 metres, the visitor reaches a first plateau with a relatively open clearing. On this cool but bright morning in the spring of 2016, the light filtering through the treetops caught the immense carpet of periwinkles covering the ground. The solitary wanderer is seized by the simple and peaceful beauty of the landscape that offers itself to him. It is hard for him to reconcile this idyllic vision with the fact that, on the afternoon of 6 June 1918, the ground was soon strewn with corpses, American and German alike. It is then that the eye is drawn to the presence here and there of large boulders as tall as a man and lying in place often in groups of two or three

– the products of the slope's erosion over hundreds of years. These were perfect natural shelters for machine guns and their crews, provided that they had lightly dug their position into the loose soil at the base of the boulders to create natural pillboxes made of stone.

These naturally protected positions could only be taken by attacking them with grenades or knives. When approaching a pile of boulders, almost every time one notices that the stone is pockmarked with bullet holes, the pattern of which reflects what had to have been the machine gun's position. The reports of those who survived the fighting, whether American or German, note the frequency and ferocity of the hand-to-hand fighting – sometimes with knives or rifle butts – that took place around these boulders.

In this wood, little more than a one-by-two-kilometre rectangle, nearly 10,000 young men, American and German, were to die in three weeks of fighting.

On the eastern side of the clearing, a road slowly descends and snakes out of the wood. It takes the visitor towards the cemetery in which the US Army buried its men from Belleau Wood and subsequent battles in the region.

The Aisne-Marne American Cemetery and Memorial holds roughly 2,000 graves. At its centre stands a monument on which are inscribed the names of a thousand missing. Even in a space as confined as Belleau Wood, the violence of the fighting made it impossible to locate identifiable remains for more than a thousand American soldiers. As soon as one enters, one encounters people outside the visitors' centre, where a permanent exhibition succinctly recounts the history of the battle (particularly insisting on the role played by the US Marines). Most are from English-speaking countries and have come to pay their respects to the marines, so many of whom lie here.

White crosses and stars of David (for Jewish soldiers) are soberly aligned on the lawn. In contrast to French, British and

German cemeteries, the crosses are not made of wood but rather of marble. The place is meticulously maintained and one spots teams of workers scrubbing the stones. On each of them is engraved the combatant's name, rank and unit. No mention of his date of birth and thus age. On each, by contrast, figures his state of origin, a reflection of American federalism. Most of the names are of Anglo-Saxon origin but a good third of them reflect the diversity of emigration to the United States. It is with some emotion that one notes a number of family names of obviously French origin, most of which seem to belong to soldiers from the state of Maine, a distant echo of the Nouvelle-France of the late eighteenth century. This is how Lucien Arsenault and Theodore Jacquet came to die in the homeland of their ancestors, in the company of George Gustaffsson, Oscar Vollrath, Hermann Levin and so many Smiths and Joneses.

All now lie together in France.

# BIBLIOGRAPHY

Audoin-Rouzeau, Stéphane, and Annette Becker, *14–18, retrouver la guerre* (Paris: Gallimard, 2000).

—— and Jean-Jacques Becker, eds, *Encyclopédie de la Grande Guerre, 1914–1918: histoire et culture* (Paris: Bayard, 2004).

Axelrod, Alan, *Miracle at Belleau Wood* (Guilford, CT: Lyons Press, 2010).

Bonk, David, *Château-Thierry and Belleau Wood 1918* (Oxford: Osprey, 2007).

Bourlet, Michael, *L'armée américaine dans la Grande Guerre 1917–1919* (Rennes: Éditions Ouest-France, 2017).

Cabanes, Bruno, *Les Américains dans la Grande Guerre* (Paris: Gallimard, 2016).

Cendrars, Blaise, *La main coupée* (1946; Paris, Denoël, 1975).

Grillot, Thomas, *Après la Grande Guerre: comment les Amérindiens des États-Unis sont devenus patriotes (1917–1947)* (Paris: Éditions de l'EHESS, 2014).

Horne, John, ed., *A Companion to World War I* (Oxford: Blackwell, 2010).

Hunter, Paul F., ed., *The Wisconsin Blue Book 1919* (Madison, WI: Democrat Printing Company, 1919).

Jünger, Ernst, *In Stahlgewittern* (printed privately, 1920). Published in English as *Storm of Steel*, trans. Michael Hofmann (London: Penguin, 2003).

Kaspi, André, *Les Américains* (Paris: Seuil, 1986).

Keene, Jennifer D., *Doughboys, the Great War, and the Remaking of America* (Baltimore, MD: John Hopkins University Press, 2001).

Lloyd, Nick, *Hundred Days: The End of the Great War* (London: Penguin, 2014).

Mead, Gary, *The Doughboys: America and the First World War* (New York: Overlook Press, 2000).

Meigs, Mark, *Optimism at Armageddon: Voices of American Participants in the First World War* (London: Macmillan, 1997).

Ministère de la guerre, État-major des Armées, *Service historique, Les armées françaises dans la Grande Guerre*, vol. vi/2 (Paris: Imprimerie Nationale, 1934).

Neiberg, Michael S., *The Path to War: How the First World War Created Modern America* (New York: Oxford University Press, 2016).

Pedroncini, Guy, *Les mutineries de 1917* (Paris: PUF, 1999).

Smith, Leonard V., *Between Mutiny and Obedience* (Princeton, NJ: Princeton University Press, 1994).

Turbergue, Jean-Pierre, ed., *La Fayette, nous voilà! Les Américains dans la grande guerre* (Triel-sur-Seine: Éditions Italiques, 2008).

Votaw, John, *The American Expeditionary Forces in World War I* (Oxford: Osprey, 2005).

Winter, Jay, ed., *The Cambridge History of the First World War*, 3 vols (Cambridge: Cambridge University Press, 2013–14).

Yockelson, Mitchell, *Forty-Seven Days: How Pershing's Warriors Came of Age to Defeat the German Army in World War I* (New York: New American Library, 2016).

# ACKNOWLEDGEMENTS

As with each of my earlier books, this work is enormously indebted to the weekly meetings of the seminar on the historiography of the First World War that I have had the privilege of following at the École des Hautes Études en Sciences Sociales (EHESS) these past fifteen years (already!). I am deeply indebted to the work of its guests and its (young and less young) participants for their various learned and enlightening contributions.

As always, I would like to give heartfelt thanks to our sensei, Stéphane Audoin-Rouzeau, an at once knowledgeable, generous and friendly mentor.

I would also like to give my thanks to Jay Winter, who has had the signal kindness of rereading and providing a foreword for this text as well as of assisting me in my first steps as a student of history by pointing me towards the EHESS.

This book also owes much to the contacts I had the privilege of making on the other side of the Atlantic. My thanks first go to Dr Monique Seefried, president of the United States World War One Centennial Commission, who gave me her time out of all proportion to my meagre academic titles. She had the kindness to steer my research very efficiently and supply me with an abundance of useful and fascinating contacts.

I would like to thank Michael Knapp and Ed Fountain at the American Battle Monuments Commission in Washington DC for warmly receiving me. Mitch Yockelson was an invaluable and friendly guide to the US National Archives at Arlington, Virginia. Finally, all of my gratitude goes to Charles Bowery for having allowed me to meet Michael Rouland, Michael DeYoung, Brian Neumann and Randy Papadopoulos, the Department of Defense's historians at the Pentagon. A very warm thanks to all of them for so kindly receiving me as well as for their deeply enriching comments.

As in the case of my two earlier books, I had the joy and privilege of working with Sophie Kucoyanis, a talented editor who is precise and warm in equal measure.

Finally, I must once again express my gratitude to Professor Emeritus Martine Segalen for her well-informed advice and patient, friendly and attentive reading of this text.

It of course goes without saying that I am alone responsible for any errors, imprecisions or omissions.

# ENDNOTES

1   It should be noted that the total population of France at that time was 39 million, of whom roughly 17 million were men (an effect of higher natural male mortality). Of this number, which ranges from newborns to the elderly, more than 8 million were mobilized. A total of 1.4 million were killed and more than 3 million wounded one or more times.

2   See Stéphane Audoin-Rouzeau and Annette Becker, 14–18, retrouver la guerre (Paris: Gallimard, 2000).

3   Jean-Michel Steg, *Death in the Ardennes: 22nd August 1914: France's Deadliest Day*, trans. Joshua Sigal (London: University of Buckingham Press, 2021) and *These Englishmen Who Died for France: 1st July 1916: The Bloodiest Day in British History*, trans. Ethan Rundell (London: University of Buckingham Press, 2022). Originally published in French as, respectively, *22 Août 1914, le jour le plus meurtrier de l'histoire de France* (Paris: Fayard, 2014), and *Ces Anglais morts pour la France: 1er juillet 1916, jour le plus meurtrier de l'histoire britannique* (Paris: Fayard, 2016).

4   See Book 5 of the *Iliad*, for example.

5   *Odyssey* xi, 15–48.

6   It is to be noted that there are doubts as to the identity of the phrase's author, which is generally attributed to Pershing's press attaché, Colonel Egbert Stanton. It is not even certain that it was truly spoken that day.

7    'Doughboys' was the term used in the American press. The
     British and French used the term 'Sammies' – a derivation
     of 'Uncle Sam' – to refer to American soldiers.

8    Of whom (only) 2 million would cross the Atlantic by 1919.

9    This committee was led by the journalist George Creel
     (1876–1953), who made full use of the resources of modern
     propaganda – press, performances, public speakers and
     posters – to advance the cause of American intervention. It
     printed more than 20 million copies of the famous 'Uncle
     Sam Wants You!' poster.

10   It is not historically unusual for a European army active far
     from its accustomed microbiological environment to suffer
     as many or more deaths from illness as from combat. Such
     was the case of the British and French armies during the
     Crimean War, and would be again for the Allies at Gallipoli,
     on the Thessaloníki front and in Mesopotamia. The meteoric
     but deadly passage of the Spanish-flu virus in the case of the
     Americans even affected army billets in the United States.
     See Jay Winter, 'La grippe espagnole', in Stéphane Audoin-
     Rouzeau and Jean-Jacques Becker, eds, *Encyclopédie de
     la Grande Guerre, 1914–1918: histoire et culture* (Paris:
     Bayard, 2004).

11   Wilson had chosen not to 'ally' the United States with the
     French and British officially, but rather to 'associate' with
     them. The country's troops could thus temporarily find
     themselves under Allied authority if US command agreed,
     but this was in no way automatic.

12   The official 'Marines' Hymn' begins as follows: 'From the
     halls of Montezuma / To the shores of Tripoli, / We fight our
     country's battles / In the air, on land and sea.'

13   The US Marine brigade consisted of two regiments, the 5th
     and 6th Marine Regiments, around 4,500 men altogether.

14   See Alan Axelrod, *Miracle at Belleau Wood* (Guilford, CT:
     Lyons Press, 2010), pp. 115–16.

15   The US Marines went into battle with a light pack on that
     morning: twenty kilograms instead of the usual forty. The
     price of this lighter burden was that they had to make do
     with less in the way of ammunition, water and bandages.
     The archival boxes of the US army for this day overflow with
     notes scribbled by officers and NCOs urgently requesting

reinforcements, supplies and above all ammunition. In particular, the French 'Chauchat' machine gun with which the US Marines were equipped required constant resupply due to its intense rate of fire.

16   National Archives and Records Administration (NARA), College Park, Maryland, 'Battle of Belleau Wood', box 140.

17   Quoted in Gary Mead, *The Doughboys: America and the First World War* (New York: Overlook Press, 2000), p. 245.

18   This episode created a great stir in the American press, which was fond of reporting these sorts of remarks.

19   Rapidly taken to the rear, he survived despite losing an eye and a part of his face. He would nevertheless return to the front three weeks later.

20   Alan Axelrod, *Miracle at Belleau Wood* (Guilford, CT: Lyons Press, 2010), p. 181.

21   Quoted in David Bonk, *Château-Thierry and Belleau Wood 1918* (Oxford: Osprey, 2007), p. 71.

22   Alan Axelrod, *Miracle at Belleau Wood* (Guilford, CT: Lyons Press, 2010), p. 229.

23   Ibid..

24   It should be recalled that the French army chalked up its highest monthly casualty tallies in the first four months of the war. Verdun, the Somme and the Chemin des Dames notwithstanding, military mortality receded in 1916 and then again in 1917.

25   Including the famous 'Lawrence of Arabia', a liaison agent to King Faisal.

26   Over the duration of the conflict, some dominions, like Canada, would resort to conscription; others, like Australia, never did so.

27   Such was the case of the young poet, Alan Seeger, one of whose last poems provides the epigraph to the present book. Upon leaving Harvard in 1910, Seeger took up residence in Paris, where he led a bohemian existence. At the outbreak of war, he immediately joined the Foreign Legion. He was killed a few days after the start of the Battle of the Somme on 4 July 1916 – American Independence Day.

28   As a matter of conviction, Quakers could not bear arms but could play humanitarian roles – as, for example, ambulance drivers.

29  Gary Mead, *The Doughboys: America and the First World War* (New York: Overlook Press, 2000), p. 41.

30  Even if 'autobiographical' accounts written long after the war ended are often of dubious veracity for various reasons. Blaise Cendrars, himself a Swiss citizen who enlisted in the Foreign Legion in August 1914, lost an arm in the fighting of 1915. See Blaise Cendrars, *La Main coupée* (1946; Paris, Denoël, 1975).

31  Ibid..

32  Faced with the convulsions set in motion by the abortive revolution of 1905, the tsarist government embarked on an actively anti-Semitic policy. This contributed to the outbreak of a series of deadly pogroms, including that of Kishinev in 1905. This persecution, in turn, energized Russia's growing Zionist movement and incited a wave of emigration, mainly to the United States.

33  For example, the fight to prohibit the sale of alcohol, which achieved success in 1920.

34  Bryan would end his career in the 1920s as the figurehead of a national campaign to outlaw the teaching of Darwin's theory of evolution in schools.

35  La Follette ultimately broke with the Republican Party and founded the Progressive Party, which he represented in the presidential election of 1924. In this capacity he received a non-negligible 15 per cent of votes.

36  British women received the right to vote in June 1918, before their American and French counterparts, who received it in 1920 and 1945, respectively.

37  Until the Second World War, Henry Ford pursued an intense campaign of isolationist propaganda in which anti-Semitism increasingly figured. He was, moreover, the only American cited by Adolf Hitler in *Mein Kampf* – quite approvingly, as it happens.

38  In August 1914, France, with its 39 million inhabitants, counted 650,000 men in its armed forces prior to mobilization. Fifteen days later, there were 3 million of them after fifteen reservist cohorts were called up. Its casualties in one week of the Battle of the Frontiers in late August 1914 exceeded the total number of troops in the American army at that time.

39 The legacy of the Spanish–American War (April–August 1898). See André Kaspi, *Les Américains* (Paris: Seuil, 1986).

40 In the course of the Civil War, conscription played only a marginal role for the Union (7.5 per cent of troops) and the Confederacy (13.5 per cent). Soldiers for the most part enlisted on a volunteer basis, joining units raised by their states of residence.

41 Alfred Mahan, *The Influence of Sea Power upon History (1660–1783)* (Boston: Little, Brown, 1890). The commander of the German *Kriegsmarine*, Admiral von Tirpitz, had Mahan's book translated and 8,000 copies distributed to all officers in his fleet.

42 Their construction had given rise to a sort of global competition, particularly with the German *Kriegsmarine* and Royal Navy.

43 In reality, the term 'preparedness' referred not just to the army but to American society as a whole, including its industry, its education and healthcare systems, and so on.

44 *Life* magazine's reports on the destruction of Louvain and its university, for instance, had a significant impact on public opinion.

45 See John Horne and Alan Kramer, *1914: les atrocités allemandes* (Paris: Tallandier, 2005) for a particularly fine-grained and well-documented analysis of the German army's extremely violent behaviour towards civilians from the beginning of the twentieth century. In 1914, practices of great cruelty first implemented against the Boxers in China (1900) and the Herero of south-west Africa (1904) would be put to work during the invasion of Belgium.

46 Doubtless more than a million French army horses and mules were killed during the conflict. See Claude Milhaud, *1914–1918: l'autre hécatombe* (Paris: Belin, 2017).

47 See 'Déclaration réglant divers points de droit maritime. Paris, 16 avril 1856'. Available at https://ihl-databases.icrc.org/dih-traites/INTRO/105.

48 See Jennifer Keene, 'North America', in Jay Winter, ed., *The Cambridge History of the First World War*, vol. i (Cambridge: Cambridge University Press, 2013–14), pp. 511–32.

49 Another very colourful figure on the American political scene at the time, Edward M. House (1858–1938) was a southern

gentleman who had sold his family's cotton plantations to get involved in finance. He was only a colonel in name, having never served in any army. He became a very close friend of Wilson, whose 1912 presidential campaign he managed, and was put up at the White House.

50    Marc-André Dufour, 'That Sinking Feeling: The U-Boot Option and German Conceptions of Victory in the First World War' [talk given at the 'War Time 2016' conference held by the International Society for First World War Studies, Oxford, November 2016].

51    The Allies were not uniquely supplied by North America. For example, Argentine producers enriched themselves in these years via massive exports of grain, meat and horses.

52    After the war, Ludendorff argued strenuously that the German army would have won the war eventually if it had not been repeatedly impaired in various ways by left-wing politicians in Germany.

53    Jennifer Keene, 'North America', in Jay Winter, ed., *The Cambridge History of the First World War*, vol. i (Cambridge: Cambridge University Press, 2013–14), p. 516.

54    A bizarre break-in at the offices of the German legation in Mexico City was mentioned to avoid alerting the Germans that Britain had succeeded in intercepting and deciphering their communications. The German minister reluctantly acknowledged the message's authenticity.

55    Those who voted against entering the war of course include the populist Republican Robert La Follette and the first woman elected to Congress, Jeannette Rankin. The latter (1880–1973) would be re-elected to the House of Representatives in 1940. A committed pacifist, she was the only member of Congress to vote against going to war after Pearl Harbor. Unsurprisingly, she devoted the last years of her life to fighting American involvement in Vietnam.

56    After Caporetto, the United States even sent a small contingent of troops to fight on the Italian front. Their contribution was of little military significance but it considerably boosted Italian morale.

57    Often cited in this connection is the exclamation by the senator Thomas Martin (who voted for declaring war) when presented with a request for an exceptional budget to equip

the American expeditionary corps: 'My God, you're not really going to send soldiers over there?'

58 Just one example: how could US soldiers be prepared to confront the use of gas when no gas masks existed on American territory in 1917, nor a single drop of poison gas?

59 A phenomenon that found particular expression in the various 'amendments' to the Constitution that, under the protection of the Supreme Court, were imposed upon the legislative branch.

60 In 1918, the age bracket was extended to cover those between eighteen and thirty-five years old.

61 Gary Mead, *The Doughboys: America and the First World War* (New York: Overlook Press, 2000), p. 70.

62 In all, volunteers represented nearly a third of all soldiers, with the remainder made up of conscripts.

63 See Bruno Cabanes, *Les Américains dans la Grande Guerre* (Paris: Gallimard, 2016).

64 See Thomas Grillot, *Après la Grande Guerre: comment les Amérindiens des États-Unis sont devenus patriotes* (1917–1947) (Paris: Éditions de l'EHESS, 2014).

65 It was at this time that he suffered a personal tragedy that would mark him for years to come: his wife and three daughters died in an accidental fire at their apartment in San Francisco's Presidio barracks.

66 Jennifer D. Keene, *Doughboys, the Great War, and the Remaking of America* (Baltimore, MD: John Hopkins University Press, 2001).

67 United States War Department, *Report of the Secretary of War to the President* (Washington DC: US Government Printing Office, 1917), p. 7.

68 As the French commander-in-chief of the time, Philippe Pétain, publicly remarked in December 1917 to those who reproached him for slowing the pace of offensive operations: 'I'm waiting for the tanks and the Americans.'

69 In addition to the prestige he enjoyed in the United States as the 'victor of the Marne', the French government and general staff were delighted to distance themselves from Joffre, who had grown embittered since being forced to leave the post of chief of general staff in December 1916 but remained extremely well connected.

70      It was in the course of this offensive that the 369th regiment, whose recruits came from New York, won the nickname of the 'Harlem Hellfighters'. Furthermore, and not insignificantly, their regimental band also distinguished itself by helping introduce jazz music to France. See Cabanes, *Les Américains dans la Grande Guerre*.

71      See Guy Pedroncini, *Les mutineries de 1917* (Paris: PUF, 1999) and Leonard V. Smith, *Between Mutiny and Obedience* (Princeton, NJ: Princeton University Press, 1994).

72      The American Congress then declared war on Austria-Hungary so that a small but symbolic number of troops could be sent to the Italian front.

73      See Ernst Jünger, *In Stahlgewittern* (printed privately, 1920). Jünger's account has been translated into English several times, most recently as *Storm of Steel*, trans. Michael Hofmann (London: Penguin, 2003).

74      Portugal entered the conflict after declaring war on Germany in March 1916.

75      Blücher was a Prussian general whose arrival on the Waterloo battlefield allowed Wellington to defeat Napoleon.

76      Gary Mead, *The Doughboys: America and the First World War* (New York: Overlook Press, 2000), p. 229.

77      Ibid.

78      Following the German advance attendant upon Operation Michael, on 29 March a German shell fell during a service at Saint-Gervais church in Paris, killing ninety-one worshippers.

79      Quoted in Mead, *The Doughboys*, p. 243.

80      Ministère de la guerre, État-major des Armées, Service historique, *Les Armées françaises dans la Grande Guerre*, vol. vi/2 (Paris: Imprimerie Nationale, 1934). Available at https://gallica.bnf.fr/ark:/12148/bpt6k6267833n.

81      Ibid., p. 244.

82      Alan Axelrod, *Miracle at Belleau Wood* (Guilford, CT: Lyons Press, 2010).

83      The platoon that brought off this critical raid was commanded by Joseph Darnand, a warrant officer. Darnand subsequently advocated collaboration with Germany and during the Second World War led the Milice Française (French Militia), a paramilitary organization created to fight the French Resistance. He ended the war in the uniform

of the Waffen-SS. Captured by the British in Italy, he was sentenced to death and executed by firing squad in August 1945.

84    Quoted in Paul F. Hunter, ed., *The Wisconsin Blue Book 1919* (Madison, WI: Democrat Printing Company, 1919), p. 323.

85    In his memoirs, Ludendorff described 19 August 1918, as 'the day of mourning for the German army'.

86    Gary Mead, *The Doughboys: America and the First World War* (New York: Overlook Press, 2000). p. xx.

87    The mistakes occurred despite the arrival of Captain George C. Marshall to oversee logistics. In 1942, he became the US Army's chief of staff.

88    This included brawls between soldiers from the two units and the arrest of Colonel (and future commander-in-chief of the Pacific) Douglas MacArthur, commanding a battalion of the 2nd Division, by the soldiers of the 1st Division.

89    The first point condemned secret diplomacy; the second demanded free maritime circulation; the third advocated free trade and the reduction of customs barriers; the fourth demanded global arms reduction; the fifth required that colonial matters be 'fairly' resolved. Eight points concerned the treatment of various territorial demands such as the return of Alsace-Lorraine to France. The fourteenth point, for its part, provided for the establishment of a 'League of Nations' that would be tasked among other things with guaranteeing the territorial integrity of its member states.

90    He only formally abdicated on 28 November.

91    The Treaty of Versailles was followed by four treaties signed with Germany's allies: the Treaty of Trianon with Hungary (June 1920); the Treaty of Saint-Germain with Austria (September 1919); the Treaty of Neuilly with Bulgaria (November 1919); and the Treaty of Sèvres with Turkey (August 1920).

92    He very likely suffered a series of mini-strokes at this time.

93    Beginning in 1921, a law was passed to impose national quotas on immigration to the United States on the basis of the fraction of the American population born abroad. This legislation was frequently tightened over the course of the 1920s and 1930s.

94   Gary Mead, *The Doughboys: America and the First World War* (New York: Overlook Press, 2000), p. 349.

95   Ibid., pp. 347–52.

96   The flu epidemic that ravaged the entire world in 1918–19 was described as 'Spanish' due to the fact that French newspapers were forbidden from mentioning its existence in the country. Its appearance and spread in a neighbouring (neutral) country could, by contrast, be reported.

97   In this domain, the parallel with the recent reluctance of former president Donald Trump and a large portion of public opinion in regards to restrictive international treaties such as the Paris Climate Accords is very striking.

98   Campaigning for his second re-election, Roosevelt even made the commitment in an election speech in Boston on 30 October 1940 never to send 'your boys' to a 'foreign war'.

99   The Lend-Lease law allowed Roosevelt to circumvent another American law that forbade selling arms to a nation at war. Lending them, by contrast…

100  A measure passed nearly unanimously; only the feminist congresswoman Jeannette Rankin, who had already voted against going to war in 1917, opposed it.